Escape
from Exclusion

Effecting

Some

Change

After

Permanent

Exclusion

An emotionally literate approach to supporting excluded and disaffected students at Key Stage 2, 3 and 4

Brian Marris and Tina Rae

Illustrated by Philippa Drakeford

Lucky Duck is more than a publishing house and training agency. George Robinson and Barbara Maines founded the company in the 1980s when they worked together as a head and psychologist developing innovative strategies to support challenging students.

They have an international reputation for their work on bullying, self-esteem, emotional literacy and many other subjects of interest to the world of education.

George and Barbara have set up a regular news-spot on the website. Twice yearly these items will be printed as a newsletter. If you would like to go on the mailing list to receive this then please contact us:

E-mail newsletter@luckyduck.co.uk   website www.luckyduck.co.uk

ISBN: 1 904 315 34 8

Published by Lucky Duck Publishing Ltd.

www.luckyduck.co.uk

Commissioning Editor: George Robinson
Editorial Team: Sarah Lynch, Mel Maines, Wendy Ogden
Illustrator: Philippa Drakeford
Designer: Helen Weller

Printed in the UK by Antony Rowe Ltd.

Acknowledgements

Brian Marris (deputy head teacher) and Tina Rae specialist educational psychologist (behaviour) would like to thank and acknowledge the support and input from the following colleagues and also the students in the current ESCAPE programme.

Lisa DeJonge	(Specialist ESCAPE teacher)
Michelle Wooley	(creative arts therapist)
Krys Wright	(group games teacher)
Alice Weston	(ESCAPE support assistant)

Thanks also to all the staff at the Hillingdon Tuition Centre who have given so much time and support in devising this programme.

Also for the support of:

Paul Helps (head teacher, Hillingdon Tuition Centre) and

Christine Sullivan (principal educational psychologist, London Borough of Hillingdon).

A note on the use of gender

Rather than repeat throughout the book the modern but cumbersome 's/he', we have decided to use both genders equally throughout the range of activities. In no way are we suggesting a stereotype for either gender in any activity. We believe that you can adapt if the example you are given does not correspond to the gender of the child in front of you!

How to use the CD-ROM

The CD-ROM contains a PDF file labelled 'Worksheets.pdf' which contains worksheets for each session in this resource. You will need Acrobat Reader version 3 or higher to view and print these resources.

The documents are set up to print to A4 but you can enlarge them to A3 by increasing the output percentage at the point of printing using the page set-up settings for your printer.

Alternatively, you can photocopy the worksheets directly from this book.

Contents

Introduction and Rationale
The ESCAPE Programme

During recent years, the government's agenda for inclusion and the focus on preventing and reducing exclusions from school have further raised awareness as to the specific needs of students with emotional, social and behavioural difficulties. Within the mainstream school context this has also led to a rethink regarding how students are both managed and supported. Under the Excellence in Cities initiative, schools have been able to further access Student Referral Units and Learning Support Units alongside setting up on-site units and introducing and implementing Pastoral Support Plans (PSPs).

Much provision is designed to support at risk students via withdrawal from mainstream lessons and contexts. Programmes have consequently been developed with the aim of providing students with opportunities to develop the social, emotional and behavioural skills that they will need in order to both access the curriculum and to succeed in the mainstream classroom context. SENCOs, Specialist Facilitators, Learning Mentors and other outside support agencies such as educational psychologists deliver many of these programmes.

Although these are laudable attempts to try and ensure the inclusion of such students, it is evident that many such approaches will not be fully effective unless they are delivered within the whole-school framework and policy for promoting positive behaviour and Emotional Literacy. While some students benefit from approaches based on cognitive behavioural and solution focused psychology, others still appear to fall through the net and fail to transfer the skills learned into the mainstream context. These are the students who may well be permanently excluded from school and consequently be required to attend a Pupil Referral Unit prior to being reintegrated into the mainstream context or accessing special provision. Programmes of support developed in the former institutions need, therefore, to build upon the good practice of mainstream staff that has previously supported such students. They will need to ensure that students really do have access to a programme of emotional, social and behavioural support from which they can gain the skills that they need. Subsequently, they should be able to successfully transfer these skills into new or more challenging environments.

It is from this rationale that the ESCAPE Programme (Effect Some Change After Permanent Exclusion) was developed within the context of a Pupil Referral Unit. Staff were keen to develop an emotionally literate approach and context in which to successfully engage with and promote change within their students.

Mental health issues and the concept of Emotional Literacy

It is important to highlight that the students for whom this programme was initially designed had all encountered many difficult situations and problems within a range of contexts. These experiences, alongside frequent rejections by significant adults, may have led to aggressive behaviours, withdrawal, volatility and some level of depression. Consequently, it would not be appropriate to label such students as mentally healthy.

A study by the Mental Health Foundation (The Big Picture, February 1999), focused upon the promotion of children and young people's mental health, defining the mentally healthy as those with the ability to:

▸ develop psychologically, emotionally, creatively, intellectually and spiritually

▸ initiate, develop and sustain mutually satisfying personal relationships

▸ use and enjoy solitude

▸ become aware of others and empathise with them

▸ play and learn

▸ develop a sense of right and wrong

▸ face problems and setbacks and learn from them in ways appropriate for the child's age.

It is important to know that, "Since the 1940s, the number of children experiencing mental ill-health has increased to one in five." (The Big Picture, 1999) This report also stated that, "Mental health problems in children and young people will continue to increase unless there is a coherent and holistic programme implemented to develop the emotional and mental health of our children... Emotionally literate children are less likely to experience mental health problems and, if they develop them, are less likely to suffer long-term. Emotional literacy is derived from a combination of parents, schools and wider social networks."(ibid).

Daniel Goleman (1995) defines Emotional Literacy as, "The capacity for recognising our own feelings and those of others, for motivating ourselves and for managing emotions well in ourselves and in our relationships."

The ESCAPE Programme was consequently an attempt to promote students' Emotional Literacy and mental health within an educational context while also promoting the notion of emotional learning as an important life long goal in every sphere of life.

To facilitate the growth of students' Emotional Literacy and their ability to promote and engender change through a process of self reflection, self-monitoring and target setting, this programme adopts a solution focused approach. This is an extremely powerful approach, which promotes change. As Rhodes and Ajimal (1995) state, "In supporting students... in their wish to change what is happening, we have found no model to approaching behaviour difficulties more useful and flexible than solution focused thinking." (P55). This is primarily because it enables those involved to formulate a new and more positive story for themselves - one in which their skills, strengths and resources can be identified and reinforced. The introductory session to the course consequently consists of an Individual Brief Therapy interview between the facilitator and the student, which focuses upon the development of solutions as opposed to the exploration of problems. A solution focused framework is provided allowing for the student to visualise 'life without the problem(s)' and to also set realistic achievable targets for the future. The 'Scaling' procedure is utilised in subsequent tutorial sessions, which provide students with a weekly forum in which to review progress and identify appropriate targets on a regular basis. These solution focused strategies are reinforced and further developed within each of the group sessions, where students are encouraged to develop solution focused problem-solving techniques via a range of co-operative activities and games.

Two types of learning

Psychologists have highlighted two types of learning - cognitive learning, which involves absorbing new data and gaining insights into existing frameworks of association, and emotional learning. The latter appears to involve engaging the part of the brain where our 'emotional signature' is stored and this invariably demands or involves new ways of thinking. For example, if most people are required to learn a new computer programme, they will probably get on with it. However, they may well offer some resistance and become upset or offended if they are told they need to improve control of their temper or anger management. According to Dann (2001), the prospect of needing to develop greater emotional intelligence is likely to generate some resistance to change. This fact has been taken into account when planning this programme, which focuses throughout on promoting, fostering and motivating students to effect change by solution focused processes and a cycle of self reflection, self monitoring and target setting. This is a continual and cyclical process involving the following process of self reflection:

What are my key skills?

What goes well and why?

What doesn't go well and why?

How can I change unhelpful patterns of behaviour?

Learning to visualise and choose a new response.

This continual process of self reflection is fostered by a combination of individual work with students, group work and the promotion of an emotionally literate learning context.

Objectives

The programme consists of weekly tutorial sessions and group sessions over a fifteen-week period. These strands of support, tutorial and activities aim to meet the following objectives:

▸ To enable students to develop an awareness of their own feelings, the ability to label these feelings and to know when they may or may not affect both work and relationships.

▸ To enable students to further develop personal insight, gaining knowledge of strengths and weaknesses and the ability to take structured criticism and feedback.

▸ To develop students' self-assurance and confidence.

▸ To encourage students to develop self-control and to particularly develop strategies to reduce stress and anxiety.

▸ To encourage students to be authentic and genuine in all contexts.

▸ To encourage students to take responsibility for behaviours and actions and to admit to mistakes and errors.

▸ To enable students to develop flexibility in order to cope more effectively with change and new ways of doing things.

▸ To ensure that students develop self-motivation and resilience.

- To raise students' self-esteem and the locus of control, that is, to encourage them to have internal control.

- To enable students to further develop and appreciate the perspectives of others, that is, empathy.

- To encourage students to become more reflective and to further develop an emotional vocabulary and the descriptive language needed to objectively describe behaviour.

- To increase self-knowledge and self-awareness.

- To encourage students to learn and make use of alternatives to physical or verbal aggression and to learn how to express their feelings and views in a positive and assertive way.

- To further develop facilitators' awareness and understanding of a range of strategies to effectively manage oneself and one's emotions.

- To encourage facilitators and support staff to adopt a consistent approach in terms of developing students' Emotional Literacy, social skills and self-esteem.

- To further enable facilitators to review the current policy and practice in terms of managing the emotional, social and behavioural needs of students in their care and to further develop healthy initiatives and programmes which promote inclusive practice for those students who present as being most at risk.

The extent to which these objectives are met is perhaps the best indicator as to the success or otherwise of this programme.

The structure of the programme

The programme is divided into fifteen sessions. Overall, the sessions aim to teach and reinforce the following key skills of Emotional Literacy:

- awareness of feelings
- personal insight
- self-assurance
- self-regulation
- authenticity
- accountability
- flexibility
- self motivation.

Each session provides a complete lesson including a games activity that aims to reinforce positive behaviour and social and emotional skills development. The fifteen sessions follow on from the initial Brief Therapy interview in which each student highlights strengths and areas for development and sets specific targets for him or herself. Students are also supported via weekly tutorial sessions that encourage self reflection and ongoing modification of these targets. A format for this tutorial session is provided in the Introductory session and this makes use of the Brief Therapy approach adopted in the Initial Interview. sessions are arranged in the following sequence:

Individual Brief Therapy interview
Session 1 - Who am I and what do I know?
Session 2 - Locus of control, Part One
Session 3 - Locus of control, Part Two
Session 4 - Managing anger, Part One
Session 5 - Managing anger, Part Two

The structure of the sessions

Each of the sessions are structured in a similar way as follows:

Aims of the session

The facilitator clarifies the main aims of the session by recording these on a flip-chart or whiteboard and talking through each point with the students in the group. This allows for the introduction of a specific skill or range of strategies to the students.

Activity sheets

Students will then be presented with a series of activity sheets that further clarify and reinforce specific skills and concepts. They may be required to work on an individual basis or in pairs or as a member of a small group. These activities aim to promote the development of personal skills and to particularly foster students' ability to co-operate and work effectively as a member of a group.

Plenary

During this part of the session the facilitator engages the students in further discussion, enabling them to feedback on their work and their responses to the activities or topics introduced in the session.

Games activity

Time for this particular aspect will need to be allocated at the facilitator's discretion. These tasks focus on the individual as part of a group and the way in which they behave as a group member. The activities are practical and often demand some element of physical movement within or outside of the classroom context.

Using the programme

These sessions can be used in a variety of ways, either with a small group or with the whole class. Although the programme has been developed within the context of a Pupil Referral Unit and subsequently used with small groups of students, it would be feasible to utilise these resources within a larger group and to adapt them as appropriate for specific groups of students.

When first trialling this programme, it was possible to allocate both the form tutor and the educational psychologist to the target group in order to deliver each of the sessions and to provide ongoing weekly tutorial support for individual students and their parents. Other members of staff were involved in delivering the games activity aspect of each session and in providing a range of therapeutic support. However, it does not necessarily follow that the same arrangements should or could be made in other contexts.

It is important to note that the allocation of such resources and attempts to work in such a multidisciplinary way need to be appropriate to each individual context. There is no 'right' way or method involved here. The most important factor is to ensure that those delivering this programme have some level of Emotional Literacy and social and behavioural skills themselves and that they are able to operate within an emotionally literate and supportive environment.

Aims

It is helpful to have the aims for each session written on to the flip-chart prior to the start of the session. This can then be on display in an accessible place in the room as students come in for the session. At this point, it is anticipated that the facilitator takes the lead in talking through each of the recorded aims. These are provided at the start of each session plan and can be adapted or altered to suit specific groups as appropriate. The aims provide the introduction to each session and clarify for students what they can expect to encounter and learn. This is an opportunity for the facilitator to field questions and clarify any new concepts or definitions with the students involved.

During Session 1 the students initially agree group rules and it is important that time is allocated so as to ensure ownership of these rules and that each student adheres to these in the subsequent sessions. It is helpful to reinforce group rules prior to clarifying the aims of each subsequent session.

Activity sheets

The facilitator can then introduce each of the activity sheets that aim to both clarify and reinforce the specific topic introduced within the session. These sheets generally require minimal amounts of recording such as drawing, writing or discussing. They can be stored in students' individual folders or files. These can be designed and made up by students prior to the start of the course or during Session 1. However, we would advise that students are provided with some time prior to the start of the course in order to make up their personal folders as this can be a time consuming activity - particularly if students are keen on presentation!

It will be important to take notice of students whose recording skills are under-developed as they will probably require additional peer or adult support. However, it is anticipated that the facilitator will be skilled in differentiation and able to ensure that all students have access to the session content regardless of level of ability. Setting up support systems and promoting paired working is a useful idea. In general, the sheets for each session demand a variety of working methods that aim to promote both independence and the ability to work appropriately with peers.

Plenary

This part of the session enables students to feedback their ideas and responses from the activity sheets. It may be useful for the facilitator to briefly summarise the main concepts covered and to record students' responses on the flip-chart or whiteboard. This will allow for highlighting experiences that may be common to the majority of students, while also reinforcing any useful and not so useful strategies or techniques covered within the session. It will also provide students with an opportunity to highlight any difficulties or concerns that they may have and to self reflect upon their own skills and the best ways of moving forwards.

Games activity

These activities aim to focus on the individual as part of a group and the ways in which they participate as a group member. The main aim is to encourage the development of appropriate social and emotional skills that will allow each student to participate and behave appropriately as a member of the team.

Each activity is presented by the facilitator at the outset. Within each session plan there is a description of the activity that can be used for this purpose. It is then suggested that the target group focus on likely problems and also agree upon rules that they may need in order to participate in the task. Once the activity has been completed it is useful to conclude with a condensed Circle Time in which students can be asked to reflect on whether the perceived problems materialised, what other problems may have occurred and what alternative ways they could have been dealt with.

If these activities are to be successful it may be necessary to allocate additional time or to be selective regarding the number of activity sheets students have access to within each session. When trialling this programme within the context of a Pupil Referral Unit, we tended to allocate additional time for this part of the session, such as tutor time. It is important to emphasise the fact that the resources are not intended to form any kind of straitjacket. Ideally, it is expected that they should be selected and adapted to suit the needs of individual groups of students and facilitators.

Looking forward

It is essential to ensure an appropriate level of support once this programme has been completed. This is true of those permanently excluded from mainstream school and in the process of reintegrating to a new context. It is also true of those students that are considered at risk in the mainstream context, and need their social, emotional and behavioural skills developing. For those students who have been targeted in withdrawal groups or as part of whole-class PSHE lessons within their mainstream schools, it may be helpful to continue to provide weekly tutorial support for targeted individuals. For those transferring from Pupil Referral Units into new mainstream contexts, support may need to be relatively intense initially and then reduced gradually as progress is made, confidence is further built and skills are evidently transferred into the new context.

This programme builds upon current good practice and initiatives for students with social, emotional and behavioural difficulties. Its basis in solution focused processes, interactivity and emotional and mental wellbeing initiatives will provide facilitators with a more dynamic and successful way forward - one that proposes a structured and accountable model built upon and centred within an emotionally literate approach.

References

Boulger, E. (2002) *Building on Social Skills*, Staffordshire, Nasen.

Casey, J. (2002) *Getting it Right: a Behaviour Curriculum*, Bristol, Lucky Duck Publishing.

Dann, J. (2001) *Emotional Intelligence in a Week*, Oxford, Hodder & Stroughton.

De Shazar, S. (1988) *Clues: Investigating Solutions in Brief Therapy*, New York, Norton.

Elias, M. J. Clabby, J. (1992) *Building Social and Emotional Development in Deaf Children, The PATH Programme*, Seattle, University of California Press.

Faupel, A., Herrick, E & Sharp, P. (1998) *Solution Talk: Hosting Therapeutic Conversations*, New York, Norton.

Goleman, E. (1995) *Emotional Intelligence - Why it can matter more that IQ*, London, Bloomsbury.

Gourley, P. (1999) *Teaching Self Control in the Classroom - a Cognitive Behavioural Approach*, Bristol, Lucky Duck Publishing.

Greenberg, M.T. & Kusche, C.A. (1993) *Promoting Social and Emotional Development in Deaf Children, The PATH Programme*, Seattle, University of California Press.

Johnson, P & Rae, T. (1999) *Crucial Skills - An Anger Management and Problem Solving Teaching Programme for High School Students*, Bristol, Lucky Duck Publishing.

Rae, T. (1998) *Dealing with Feeling*, Bristol, Lucky Duck Publishing.

Rae, T. (2000) *Confidence, Assertiveness, Self-Esteem - a Series of Twelve Sessions for Secondary School Students*, Bristol, Lucky Duck Publishing.

Rae, T. (2001) *Strictly Stress - Effective Stress Management for High School Students*, Bristol, Lucky Duck Publishing.

Rhodes, J. & Ajimal, Y. (1995) *Solution Focused Thinking in Schools*, London, Brief Therapy Publication.

Sheldon, B. (1995) *Cognitive Behavioural Therapy: Research, Practice and Philosophy*, London, Routledge.

Wardle, C. & Rae, T. (2002) *School Survival - Helping Students Survive and Succeed in Secondary School*, Bristol, Lucky Duck Publishing.

Warden, E. & Christie, D. (1997) *Teaching Social Behaviou*r, London, David Fulton Publishers.

White, M. (1999) *Picture This - Guided Imagery for Circle Time*, Bristol, Lucky Duck Publishing.

Introductory Session

Individual Brief Therapy Interview

Aims of the session

This introductory session consists of a one-to-one interview between each student and the course facilitator. The interview will probably last 45 minutes to one hour and should allow the student to focus upon what actually works as opposed to what's going wrong, that is, the development of a collaborative ethos. The central aim is to help the student define some achievable goals and to clarify the practical resources and strategies that may be required in order to achieve such goals.

The facilitator needs to ensure that this interview can take place in a quiet, comfortable and private location. Students need to be made aware that this is a confidential interview and that views will not be related to anyone else. Any exception to such a rule would be at the student's own request or if the student should disclose any information that may be perceived to put them at risk. In the latter instance, the course facilitator would need to clarify this fact with the student prior to the start of the interview and adhere to the usual child protection rules and regulations within the existing context.

This initial interview follows a solution focused brief therapy approach and focuses upon the development of solutions as opposed to the exploration of problems. It is hoped that this session would also allow for some quality time between the course facilitator and the student and allow both to begin to build up a positive and trusting relationship. It is the course facilitator's job to record the student's responses on the form and this may be done in note form or in whatever way is most comfortable to the individual concerned. It is important that the student's views are recorded and that the course facilitator does not in any sense speak for the student or attempt to alter his words.

Resources

The following resources will be needed for the one-to-one interviews:

- a quiet private room
- 45 minutes to one hour approximately per interview
- a photocopy of the brief therapy format
- a photocopy of the scaling activity format
- a photocopy of the tutorial format.

Part One - Brief Interview 1

The first part of the interview focuses on the following questions:

- ▸ What is currently going well for you in your life and why?

- ▸ What is currently not going so well for you in your life and why?

- ▸ What is currently going well at home and why?

- ▸ What is currently not going quite so well at home and why?

- ▸ What do you think might help you both at home and at school?

Part Two- Brief Interview 2

In this second part of the interview the student is asked the Miracle Question. This requires the student to imagine herself in a situation in which all her problems, negative feelings and difficulties are 'solved'. She is asked to describe a perfect day in which everything goes well both at home and at school. The question may be presented in the following way,

> "Imagine that you go to bed tonight and a miracle happens! Someone or something waves a magic wand over you and in that instant all of your problems and difficulties are solved. You wake up to the most perfect day possible both at home and at school. What is different? Have a think. How does your day begin and then go on? Talk through what happens on this ideal or magic day step by step right from the moment you open your eyes to the moment you go back to bed in the evening."

Utilising this Miracle Question is central to this initial interview process and aims to enable the students to begin to visualise 'life without the problem'. (de Shazer 1998, Furman & Ahola, 1992). Once the students begin to talk about life 'without the problem', it is hoped that they can then begin to identify and formulate suggestions and ideas as to how they may start to make changes in their lives. Students should also be more comfortable in identifying and formulating appropriate and achievable personal goals at this point. By identifying how this is different to a usual day, students can quickly begin to see some of the very small changes that they might be able to make which will begin to make a very real difference to their lives on a daily basis. When the facilitator asks this Miracle Question, it is important to emphasise to students that such an ideal or magic day does not preclude them from attending school. The idea is for them to describe school as they would actually like it to be. This is an extremely powerful tool in terms of encouraging the visualisation of life as it could be. As Rhodes & Ajmal 1995 suggest,

> "In supporting students, teachers and parents in their wish to change what is happening, we have found no model approaching behaviour difficulties more useful and flexible that solution focused thinking. It enables a different story to be told, one which emphasises the skills, strengths and resources of those involved." (Rhodes J & Ajmal Y 1995 - Page 55)

For some students this will not be a particularly easy task, particularly when they have a wealth of negative experiences and relationships behind them. However, it is hoped that within this private, comfortable and secure framework in which the positives are emphasised and highlighted, students will be able to begin to see the possibility of effecting real change and obtaining better outcomes for themselves.

> **Example: Patrick (13 years)**
>
> Patrick said that he always had a bad time at school because generally the teachers didn't like him. They always seemed to expect him to behave badly and this meant that he got angry very quickly and didn't want to give them a chance to teach him. Consequently, he'd muck around, shout out and generally try to disrupt their lessons. He said that his mum and dad were always angry with him because they always got phone calls from the school and he'd been excluded so many times. They said that he was just a disaster and would never make anything of his life. Patrick was always getting into trouble after school as well, as he tended not to go straight home but would hang around with his mates, get involved in recreational drug use and the odd bit of shoplifting. Patrick recognised that he would find it very difficult to get back into a mainstream school unless he could try and 'sort himself out'.

When looking at how his miracle day was different to a usual day, it became very obvious that he actually wanted to succeed and do well in many of his lessons but that he was now too frightened to give himself or the teachers a chance.

In order to begin to make some of the necessary changes, Patrick agreed that he needed to do the following:

▶ Learn how to stop and think before opening his mouth, particularly when people had just said something challenging to him.

▶ Sit at the front of the class so that he could be seen by the teacher and wasn't so tempted to engage in chat with others at the back.

▶ Go home straightaway from school so that he could have something to eat, see his mum and avoid getting into trouble.

▶ Try to think of the teachers as being human beings rather than aliens from another planet and recognise that they have feelings too.

▶ Ask for time out if he gets angry or thinks that he can't cope in a certain situation in class.

▶ Start thinking about what he really wanted to do in the future and to start talking about this with his mum and dad.

Once the students have answered the questions and completed the activities in Parts One and Two of the one-to-one interview, they can then proceed to complete the Scaling Activity (Part Three).

Part Three - The Scaling Activity

This activity asks the students to rate themselves on a scale of 1-10 for how they are generally feeling about their lives at that moment. 1 would indicate that they felt extremely negative about life in general, including school life, 5 would indicate that they felt generally okay but recognised the need to make some improvements and 10 would imply that things couldn't be better, that is they were perfect!

The rating or scaling system can be explained to students prior to the start of the activity and once the rating has been recorded, students can further reflect upon the following questions:

▶ What have you done to get this point?

▶ Where would you like to get to on this scale?

- How can you do this?

- What are your targets?

These personal targets need to be realistic and achievable and negotiated between both the student and the course facilitator.

Example: Irene (14 years)

"I am on 4. This is because I have got excluded permanently from two schools and my behaviour has been pretty bad. I have got into a lot of trouble because I can't seem to manage my temper very well and I've got into fights and have been smoking a lot. My mum is really fed up with me and has grounded me for the last two months because my behaviour was so bad in the last school and she is so ashamed of me."

I have been trying quite hard with my work though and I have caught up with a lot of coursework over the last four weeks. I have also got two very good friends who have stood by me through all this.

I would like to be on 8 or 9. I can do this by:

- trying to control my anger more

- stopping and thinking before reacting

- planning for the future and making a career plan that is definite

- concentrating in class

- not getting angry and shouting back at teachers but holding on so that I can talk to them later if there is a problem

- talking about problems rather than bottling them up."

Tutorials - Weekly Record Form

Once students have completed the scaling activity, the facilitator can briefly explain the use of the Weekly Record Form for tutorial sessions. A solution focused process is used in order to provide a supportive structure for students throughout the duration and subsequent to the completion of this course. The idea is to review progress on a weekly basis (including specific targets) and to then identify targets for the coming week.

This kind of system allows the students to work consistently with a significant adult in the school or unit context with whom they can then build up a trusting and positive relationship. The idea is to also allow for the regular setting of appropriate, achievable targets and for the student to be encouraged to become more reflective and to develop a greater range of personal coping strategies. Hopefully then, if things should go wrong, it should always be possible to re-establish and maintain a positive solution focused approach. Before the end of this initial one-to-one interview, the course facilitator and the student should arrange a time to complete the Tutorial Weekly Record Form and to subsequently commit to a regular time in which to review progress and set new, realistic and achievable goals. The latter will, hopefully, also be informed by the course content and the concepts and strategies presented to the students throughout the 15-session programme.

Initial Brief Therapy Interview

Name of student: [   ]

Year group: [   ]

Date of interview: [   ]

Recorded by: [   ]

ESCAPE →

Brief Interview

What is currently going well for you in your life?

Why?

What is currently not going so well for you in your life?

Why?

What is currently going well at home?

Why?

What is currently not going quite so well at home?

Why?

What do you think might help you at home?

...at school?

Brief Interview 2

Imagine that you go to bed tonight and a miracle happens – someone or something waves a magic wand over you and all your problems and difficulties are solved. You wake up to a perfect stress-free day – at home and at school. What is different? Think. How does your day begin and then go on?

Talk through what happens on this magic day.

What is different to a 'usual day'? Let's think back and list the differences.

Scaling Activity

Highlight where you are now on the scale. Your score will show how you feel about your life at the moment.

A score of   1 =   you feel very down and negative and things are not going well

                5 =   reasonably OK

            10 =   you feel brilliant and things couldn't be better.

```
1      2      3      4      5      6      7      8      9      10
|||||||||||||||||||||||||||||||||||||||||||||||||||||||||||||||||||
```

What have you done to get to this point?

Where would you like to get to on the scale?

How can you do this?

What are you targets?

Weekly Tutorial Record

Name _____ Date _____

On a scale of 1 to 10, where am I now in terms of meeting my targets this week?

    1 = very negative

    5 = OK

    10 = brilliant

1	2	3	4	5	6	7	8	9	10

What has gone well this week?

What hasn't gone quite so well?

Where would I like to be on the scale this time next week?

In order to get there my targets will be:

1. _____

2. _____

3. _____

4. _____

I will review my targets on _____ with _____

Signed _____ _____

                Pupil   Tutor

Session 1

Who am I and what do I know?

Aims of the session

As described in the introduction, the facilitator can record the main aims of the session on the whiteboard or flip-chart prior to pupils entering the room. In this session these are as follows:

▸ for the facilitator to clarify the reasons why we are
   all here and what the course is all about

▸ for students to understand what the process of exclusion actually
   involves and what the consequences of being excluded may be

▸ for students to be able to articulate the reasons for their own exclusions

▸ for students to identify and articulate the preferred future
   or the most positive outcomes for themselves

▸ for students to be able to set personal targets for the coming 15 week period and
   to identify long-term goals for themselves which are realistic and achievable.

It will be important for the facilitator to clarify the contents of the course and to discuss with students the main aims and objectives that they have identified for the next 15-week period. Central to this will be the notion of students effecting change within themselves and accepting the need to do so. Initially this may be quite a difficult concept for some students to cope with as there may well be a propensity to resort to blaming others or the previous or current context in which they find themselves. It is consequently extremely important to clarify that this is intended as a positive programme of support which will, hopefully, encourage and enable each individual to reach their own goals and achieve their own potential, alongside effecting some very real and positive changes, both emotionally and academically. It is also important to highlight that it would be important to create a positive climate in which students can begin to support each other in this process of change. The facilitator might highlight the following objectives:

▸ to provide each student with private listening time and space in which
   they can reflect on both their feelings and their behaviours

▸ to help students develop and make use of strategies for
   controlling anger and managing stress more effectively

▸ to encourage students to become more reflective regarding their own
   situation and to understand that they can really effect change

▸ to encourage students to recognise their right to be who they are and to
   be accepted by others and the importance of accepting difference

- ‣ to encourage students to develop self-help strategies in order to cope with conflict and difficult situations

- ‣ to increase students' ability to socialise and co-operate within a group and to support and empathise with others.

Once these objectives have been discussed and students have been given the opportunity to clarify and raise pertinent issues, it will be necessary to proceed to the first activity that involves setting group rules.

Activity sheet - Our Group Rules

Setting the group rules clearly leads on from the initial discussion of the course objectives. It is essential that students have time to agree and discuss their own set of rules so as to ensure ownership of them and that everyone in the group or class adheres to them in each of the subsequent sessions. Group rules may include the following:

- ‣ We agree to keep our discussion private to the group and not chat about it with others outside of the group.

- ‣ We will all try to make some kind of contribution that is positive and think of ideas in each session.

- ‣ We will not put each other down or make fools of each other.

- ‣ We will try to work together and respect each other's point of view.

- ‣ We will try to look after each other and back each other up.

- ‣ No-one in our group will be made to say anything if they don't want to.

- ‣ We won't use put-downs.

Activity sheet - How much do I know about exclusions?

This can either be done on an individual basis or in pairs or as a whole group or class activity. The facilitator can make an assessment as to which is the most appropriate arrangement for any given group. It is useful to draw this activity together via a mini plenary, that is, allowing students to feedback verbally with the facilitator acting as a scribe, as opposed to requiring each student to record information on the sheet. The sheet is merely intended to act as a prompt. Once student responses have been gathered, the facilitator can feedback the accurate information. The questions and answers are as follows:

What is a fixed term exclusion?

A set number of days, not to exceed 45 in a year.

What is a permanent exclusion?

Exclusion from the school indefinitely, requires verification of the School Pupil Disciplinary Sub Committee within 15 school days.

How many pupils were excluded from school between 2001 and 2002?

1997/98	1998/99	1999/00	2000/01	2001/02
12,298	10,438	8,323	9,135	9,535

How old were most of the pupils?

> 66 per cent were of pupils aged 13, 14 or 15
>
> 22 per cent were of pupils aged 13,
>
> 27 per cent of pupils aged 14
>
> 17 per cent of pupils aged 15.

Why do you think more pupils were excluded at these ages?

> Possibly due to hormones and their effect upon behaviour, the fact that SATs are undertaken or students are preparing for exams.

Are more boys excluded than girls, if so why?

> Yes. Approximately 83% are boys and this may be due to boys exhibiting more aggressive and physical behaviours.

How many excluded pupils go back to mainstream school?

> Depends upon their age. The majority of Key Stage 2, approximately half of Key Stage 3 and a few Key Stage 4 students.

What happens to most excluded pupils in their later lives?

> They may have a poor job record, low income or custodial sentences.

(Information from: www.statistics.gov.uk)

The intention is to dispel any myths around this issue and to particularly reinforce that being excluded permanently from any school is an extremely serious matter. However, it is vital that each of the students involved recognises the positives can follow negatives and that they will always be in a position to effect change and to gain a better outcome for themselves in their lives. Visualising a better future can prompt part of this latter process. Consequently, the next activity encourages students to visualise a more ideal self and to articulate the qualities of such a being.

Activity sheet - This is how I would really like to be

The students are asked to draw themselves within the picture frame and to then record the qualities around the outside of the picture frame. Students can identify a range of positive qualities that they would like to have in the future or that they feel they may be beginning to develop at the moment. This is also an opportunity to visualise a positive future and to further clarify qualities that they would like to change in themselves and to ultimately reject.

Activity sheet - My personal target sheet

This sheet requires students to utilise a scaling activity in order to identify four specific targets for the coming 15 weeks. These may well be similar to those identified in the Initial Brief Therapy Interview. However, having now identified an ideal self it may be that students' targets become slightly more ambitious. They will also be asked to identify others who may be able to help them achieve these targets alongside clarifying how they can help themselves in order to achieve their goals. This reflective and cyclical process is something which students will then be required to do throughout the course, both in the group sessions and in individual tutorial sessions. Most important is the notion of visualising a preferred future and being extremely specific about how and when they will know they have achieved their goals, that is, what will be different and how they will feel about it.

Plenary

As in the introduction to the session, the facilitator can make use of the whiteboard or flip-chart in order to act as a scribe for students' views and responses. This part of the session aims to review the session contents and ask, 'What have we learnt?' This will be an opportunity to reinforce the agreed group rules and to say that these will stand for the remainder of the course. Students can also summarise their knowledge, both new and old, about exclusions and they can, share their own personal targets. The reinforcement of the group rules will, of course, be extremely important in terms of acceding to the following games activity which aims to promote co-operative skills and to reinforce social and emotional learning.

Games activity - White Water

Organise students into groups of four. Give each group two sheets of A1 paper. This is large enough to stand on but small enough to encourage students to hold onto and support each other.

The groups are required to cross a rapid flowing river, using their two 'stepping stones'. Nobody is allowed to step into the water so the group must retrieve a 'stepping stone' while standing on the other. A distance of five to six metres and objects to identify the banks of the river helps to clarify the task.

The course facilitator can describe the activity and field any questions from students while also facilitating a final Circle Time as to how the activity went. It may be useful to consider the following questions:

How did we feel about this activity initially?
What kinds of problems did we think would occur?
What problems actually materialised?
How did we deal with these difficulties?
Could we have dealt with them more effectively?
How will we deal with them better next time?
What do we think we learnt from this activity?

These questions can be utilised to facilitate group reflections and problem-solving in all subsequent sessions.

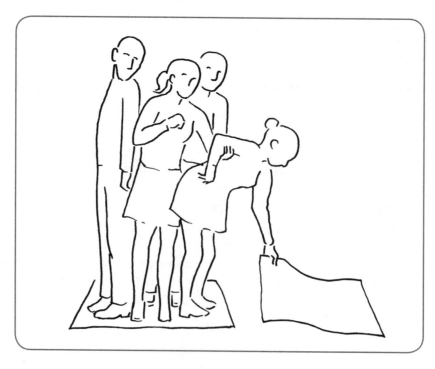

Our group rules

The do's and don'ts of being in the ESCAPE group

We all agree to abide by our rules:

▶

▶

▶

▶

▶

▶

Signed _____ date _____

How much do I know about exclusions?

▶ What is a 'fixed term' exclusion?

▶ What is a permanent exclusion?

▶ How many pupils were excluded from school between 2001 and 2002? Try to estimate the figure.

▶ How old were most of the pupils?

▶ Why do you think more pupils were excluded at this age?

▶ Are more boys excluded than girls, if so why?

▶ How many excluded pupils go back to mainstream school?

▶ What happens to most excluded pupils in their later lives?

Exclusions Answers

▶ What is a 'fixed term' exclusion?
A set number of days, not to exceed 45 in a year.

▶ What is a permanent exclusion?

Exclusion from the school indefinitely, requires verification of the School Pupil Disciplinary Sub Committee within 15 school days.

▶ How many pupils were excluded from school between 2001 and 2002?

1997/98	1998/99	1999/00	2000/01	2001/02
12,298	10,438	8,323	9,135	9,535

▶ How old were most of the pupils?

66 per cent were of pupils aged 13, 14 or 15 ;
22 per cent were of pupils aged 13,
27 per cent of pupils aged 14
17 per cent of pupils aged 15.

▶ Why do you think more pupils were excluded at this age?

Possibly due to hormones and their effect upon behaviour or because SAT.s are undertaken or students are preparing for exams.

▶ Are more boys excluded than girls, if so why?

Approximately 83% are boys and this may be due to boys exhibiting more aggressive and physical behaviours.

▶ How many excluded pupils go back to mainstream school?

Depends upon their age; majority of Key Stage 2, approximately half Key Stage 3 and a few Key Stage 4 students.

▶ What happens to most excluded pupils in their later lives?

They may have a poor job record, low income and custodial sentences.

This is how I would really like to be

Draw yourself and record your qualities around the outside of the picture frame.

I don't want to be like:

My personal target sheet

Name _____   Date _____

On a scale of 1 to 10, where am I now in terms of how positive I feel about my situation and myself?

(1 = very negative   5 = OK   10= brilliant)

```
1      2      3      4      5      6      7      8      9      10
|⊥⊥⊥⊥|⊥⊥⊥⊥|⊥⊥⊥⊥|⊥⊥⊥⊥|⊥⊥⊥⊥|⊥⊥⊥⊥|⊥⊥⊥⊥|⊥⊥⊥⊥|⊥⊥⊥⊥|
```

Where would I like to be on the scale?   [   ]

In order to get there my targets will be:

1 _____

2 _____

3 _____

4 _____

▶ Who can help me achieve these targets and how?

▶ How can they help me?

▶ How can I help myself?

▶ When will I know that I've reached my goals?

▶ What will be different?

▶ How will I feel?

Now go for it!

34

Session 2

Locus of Control - Part One

Aims of the session

As described in the introduction, the facilitator can record the main aims of the session on the whiteboard or flip-chart prior to pupils entering the room. In this session these are as follows:

- for students to understand the concept of locus of control

- for students to be able to distinguish between 'being in control' and 'not being in control' in a range of different situations

- for students to understand the need to accept responsibility for their behaviours and for the consequences of those behaviours

- for students to be able to self reflect and identify situations when they have been in control and when they have blamed others for their behaviour.

It will initially be important for the facilitator to ensure that students have grasped the concept of locus of control. This will involve explaining the distinction between external and internal control. Students need to understand that if they blame others or the context for their behaviour then the control is external, whereas if they accept responsibility for what they have done and the choices that they have made, then they will have internal control. This is an extremely important concept and all students need to be made aware of the need to develop and maintain such internal control as this is what ultimately provides them with their power. To accept a position of external control will simply disempower the student yet again.

The facilitator can make use of a couple of scripts in order to illustrate this distinction initially. For example, "I did well in the maths test because I worked hard and revised a lot," shows an internal locus of control because the student is taking responsibility for revising and for the outcome of that revision, that is, 'it was down to me'. "I did well on the test because it was easy," shows an external locus of control because the student is saying that he had no control over the test and that his input was irrelevant, that is, it was simply down to the test being easy!

Once the facilitator has clarified this distinction, the students can then proceed to the first activity sheet that encourages them to make their own decisions regarding a range of statements.

The following statements are categorised as indicating external or internal control:

I did well in the test because I worked hard.	(internal control)
The sums were too hard for me so I failed.	(external control)
The lesson was boring so I got sent to another class.	(external control)
The teacher was in a bad mood so she sent me out.	(external control)
I got a good report because the teachers are nicer.	(external control)
I scored three goals because the goalkeeper was rubbish.	(external control)
I got in trouble because the teacher wasn't strict enough.	(external control)
My mum likes my brother more than me so I act up at home.	(external control)
I shouted at my mate so Miss sent me out.	(internal control)
The teacher only likes boffins so she ignored me and I lost my temper.	(external control)

Activity sheet - Make Your Decision

Each student can be provided with a copy of this particular activity sheet although paired working can be encouraged. Students are required to read through a range of statements and to identify those which show the student being in control and those which show others being in control or the student blaming others. Students are asked to colour code each of the statements and then to identify how many of the statements show internal control and how many show external control.

It is helpful to encourage students to feedback straight after having completed this activity to ensure that all involved understand the distinction.

Activity sheet - Resource Cards

Students are provided with a series of 24 statements. It will be helpful for the facilitator to have prepared these statements prior to the start of the session. The two sheets (each containing 12 statements) can be photocopied onto A4 card. The statements are then cut out and mixed up to ensure a mix of internal and external control statements. The students then sort the cards into two piles - those that show or reveal internal control or external control. This is a very practical activity and students may wish to do it as a group activity rather than working in pairs or on an individual basis. The former would encourage more discussion and students would be able to articulate personal views and responses here.

Activity sheet - My own locus of control

This activity requires students to reflect upon their own level of internal control and to identify two occasions on which they had internal control and two on which they had external control. They are then required to consider which was the most uncomfortable situation and why and which was the most comfortable situation and why. It is helpful to encourage students to share their ideas briefly and to compare notes as to any similarities and differences in their experiences. It is important throughout each of these activities to ensure that students understand the distinction and are beginning to hear themselves making use of internal control. For example, when they hear themselves saying, "The teacher was being horrible to me," they will be able to reflect further upon this statement and quickly identify it as being a statement of external control. The aim is to develop these thought processes and scripts more and more so that they can impact upon the classroom and be transferred from this smaller group into a larger context.

Plenary

The facilitator can make use of the whiteboard in order to gather feedback from the students alongside summarising the main concepts and strategies learnt in this session. It is helpful to address the following questions:

- What have we learnt?
- What is the locus of control?
- Do we have internal control and can we provide examples of this?
- Do we have external control sometimes and can we provide examples of this?
- Why is it important to develop locus of control?

Games activity - Numbered Chairs

Each group of students is provided with five plastic stacking chairs numbered one to five. These are stacked in ascending order with chair one at the bottom.

Place three hula-hoops on the floor in a line and the stack of chairs in the first hoop. The object of the game is to move the chairs and stack them in the third hoop, in ascending order with chair one at the bottom. The catch is that the chairs can only be moved one by one and at no time is a chair with a lower number able to be stacked on a chair with a higher number (for example, chair two can not be stacked on chair five). It doesn't matter about the order the hoops are used in and chairs can (and will have to) be moved in each direction. The solution is provided overleaf.

- How did we feel about this activity initially?
- What kinds of problems did we think would occur?
- What problems actually materialised?
- How did we deal with these difficulties?
- Could we have dealt with them more effectively?
- How will we deal with them better next time?
- What do we think we learnt from this activity?

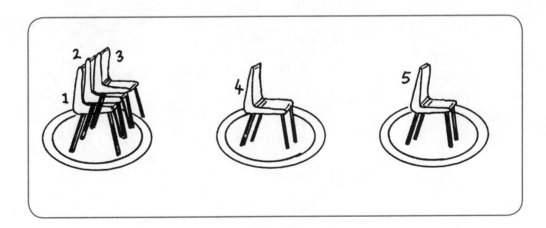

Solution:

The first hoop is Hoop A

The second hoop is Hoop B

The third hoop is Hoop C.

Move Chair (C) 5 to Hoop (H) C.

Move C4 to HB

C5 to HA

C4 to HC.

C5 to HC.

C3 to HB.

C5 to HB

C4 to HA

C5 to HA.

C3 to HC.

C5 to HC.

C4 to HB.

C5 to HA.

C4 to HC.

C5 to HC.

C2 to HB.

C5 to HA.

C4 to HB.

C5 to HB.

C3 to HA.

C5 to HA.

C4 to HC.

C5 to HC.

C3 to HB.

C5 to HA.

C4 to HB.

C5 to HB.

C1 to HC.

C5 to HC.

C4 to HA.

C5 to HA.

C3 to HC.

C5 to HC.

C4 to HB.

C5 to HB.

C3 to HA.

C5 to HC.

C4 to HA.

C5 to HA.

C2 to HC.

C5 to HC.

C4 to HB.

C5 to HB.

C3 to HC.

C5 to HA.

C4 to HC.

C5 to HC.

Make Your Decision

Name _____   Date _____

Who is in control? Colour the following quotes.

Red for pupil in control:

Blue is for others in control or the pupil blaming others.

The sums were too hard for me so I failed

I scored three goals because the goalkeeper was rubbish

I did well in the test because I worked hard

I scored a goal because I concentrated

I got into trouble because the teacher wasn't strict enough

My mum likes my brother more than me so I act up at home

I got a good report because the teachers are nicer

I shouted at my mate so Miss sent me out

The teacher was in a bad mood so she sent me out

The lesson was boring so I got sent to another class

The teacher only likes boffins so she ignored me and I lost my temper

How many statements show internal control?

How many statements show external control?

Resource Cards

I did well in the English exam because I worked hard.	I scored a goal because I concentrated.
I was picked for the team because I tried hard.	I got extra pocket money because I cleaned the kitchen.
I got a merit because I tried hard all day.	I bumped into him because I wasn't concentrating.
I came first in the race because I ran the fastest.	I wasn't allowed to go to the games session because I misbehaved in English.
I wasn't allowed to play pool at break time because I was late for school this morning.	I was late for school because I ignored my alarm.
I pushed in the bus queue so the driver made me get off the bus.	I bullied the boy because I wanted his mobile phone.

More Resource Cards

He did better than me because he's clever and the teacher likes him more.	She made me miss the goal because she shouted just before I was about to kick.
He's mean and so he said I couldn't have a merit.	She didn't pick me for the team because she was in a bad mood.
She bumped into me on purpose because she doesn't like me.	He took my pocket money away because the house was a mess and he said it was my fault.
She beat me in the race because she cheated.	He stopped me going to the games session because he likes to upset people.
My mum made me late for school because she wouldn't get me up.	The bus driver was rude to me because he doesn't like kids.
The shopkeeper accused me of stealing because he's racist.	They made me bully that boy.

My own locus of control

Stop, think and reflect! When were you in control and when did you blame others? Try to identify four examples below:

I had internal control when

I had external control when

I had internal control when

I had external control when

Which was the most uncomfortable situation and why?

_____

_____

Which was the most comfortable situation and why?

_____

_____

Session 3

Locus of Control - Part Two

Aims of the session

The facilitator can outline the aims of the session to students in the group, making use of a whiteboard. For this session these will be as follows:

▸ for students to identify the reasons why they were excluded from school

▸ for students to begin to objectively describe their behaviour and to be able to reflect upon their behaviours

▸ to reinforce the concept of locus of control and the distinction between internal and external control

▸ for students to begin to understand how they can support each other in terms of changing and coping more effectively with their behaviours and feelings.

It would be helpful to refer back to the previous session and to ask students to contribute to revising the concept of locus of control. It will also be important to emphasise the need to be supportive of each other and to further develop the ability to empathise with one another. One strength of working within the group context is the way in which the group can develop as a support structure and highlight and reinforce the students' ability to proactively support and monitor each other's behaviours. This will be particularly important in this session when students will be discussing the reasons for their own exclusions from school and attempting to clarify and identify future targets for themselves. For many students, the initial activity will be quite a challenging one and it is important for the facilitator to ensure that this takes place within a supportive context.

Activity sheet - The Exclusion Interview

This activity requires students to reflect upon their own experiences and to work in pairs in order to interview each other and elicit information. It is helpful for students to think of this in terms of a radio or television interview. They can make use of tape recorders to record the interviews. Students may wish to 'practise' prior to recording. This should be at the discretion of the facilitator and the students involved in the group. It is important to emphasise that this is not intended to be a threatening experience but rather one in which students can learn the importance of self reflection and the ways in which mistakes can be learnt from. The aim is to be solution focused and identifying a way forward for each of the individuals involved. The nine questions are as follows:

1. What school did you go to?
2. What did you like about it?
3. What didn't you like about it?
4. Do you miss anything about your old school?
5. Why did you get excluded? What happened?

6. How do you feel about this now?
7. Do you think you could have done anything different?
8. Do you want to go back to your old school?
9. How do you think you can get back into school now?

The latter two questions may raise some concerns with students and it is important to be very clear about their individual positions, that is, some students may be planning on going back to their previous school while others who have been permanently excluded may be awaiting a new school placement. It is important that students realise the importance of being honest and accepting responsibility for their own behaviours while also acknowledging the ways in which the context may have both helped and hindered them in the past.

Activity sheet - Interview Analysis

In this activity students can work in their pairs and listen carefully to the taped interview that they have conducted. They are asked to think carefully about the language used in the interview and to identify whether each person has internal or external control. This focus can initially be upon whether they have accepted responsibility for the outcomes of their behaviours. Students are required to write down four sentences from each of the interviews and then to sort these into two columns on the worksheet - one for internal control and one for external control. For example, when discussing the reasons for their exclusion that may include inappropriate behaviours, a student may say, "I pushed the chair over because I got angry," and this would be placed in the internal control column while another student may say, "Mrs Perrona was in a mood so she made me push the chair over." The latter statement would come under the external control column.

The final part of this activity requires students to analyse whether they think they have internal or external control at the current time. They then need to consider what they think they should be doing now in order to gain more internal control and a greater ability to manage their behaviour effectively. If the group is particularly secure in terms of relationships at this stage, it may be useful to swap tapes and allow another pair to analyse the statements made by two of their peers. This is at the discretion of the facilitator and any such arrangement would need to reflect the current needs of the group.

Plenary

The facilitator can make use of the whiteboard to encourage students to feedback their responses as to how helpful or otherwise they found the two activities. It is particularly useful to reflect on the kinds of feelings that were engendered by participating in this experience. For example: Did the students find this challenging? Did they feel angry or resentful? Did recalling previous events bring back difficult and uncomfortable emotions? Do they think they have come to terms with what has happened to them in the past? How do they think they will be able to cope more effectively in the future in order to achieve a better outcome for themselves?

It is also helpful to reflect upon the language used within this session and to ensure that all students have an understanding of each of the following concepts:

- peer support
- self-reflection
- internal and external control
- best possible outcome
- empathy
- self-regulation.

Games activity - Co-operative Ski

Students, in groups of three, are provided with two planks of wood, approximately 1800mm x 180mm and six pieces of string about two metres long. They are required to make a pair of 'skis' and to 'ski' a defined distance. To achieve this the students will need to tie their feet to the 'skis' either directly or by making loops. They will need to move by lifting alternate feet and hence the ski. It's not as easy as it sounds and they will have to co-operate!

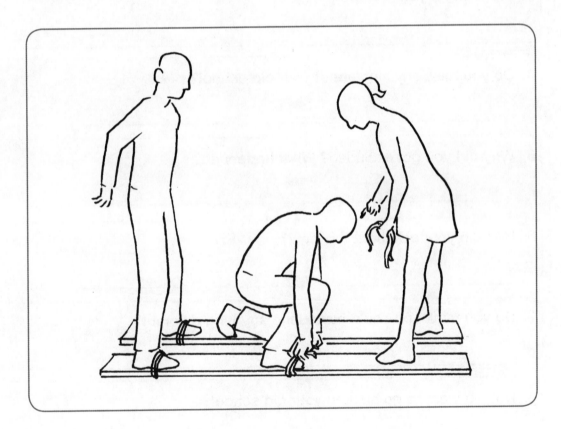

The Exclusion Interview

Time to tell your own story! Work in pairs. Take it in turns to ask these questions of each other. Tape your talks.

1. What school did you go to?

2. What did you like about it?

3. What didn't you like about it?

4. Do you miss anything about your old school?

5. Why did you get excluded? What happened?

6. How do you feel about this now?

7. Do you think you could have done anything different?

8. Do you want to go back to your old school?

9. How do you think you can get back into school now?

Interview Analysis

Work in pairs and listen carefully to the taped interview. Think carefully about the language used by the student.

Do they have internal or external control?

Do they accept responsibility for the outcomes? Write four sentences from the interviews.

Internal Control	External Control
I pushed the chair over because I got angry	Mrs Perrona was in a mood so she made me push the chair over
1	1
2	2
3	3
4	4

Stop and think.

How many sentences did you record on each side? Do you think the students have internal or external control at the moment? What do you think they should be doing now?

Session 4
Managing Anger - Part One

Aims of the session

The facilitator can record the aims for the session on the whiteboard or flip-chart prior to students entering the room. This can then be used as a prompt for the initial discussion in which these are outlined and explained to students who also have the opportunity to question and clarify any points for themselves. The main aims of the session are as follows:

- for students to be able to identify personal triggers to anger

- for students to understand how anger is often a secondary emotion, that is coming after feelings such as fear, jealousy or humiliation

- for students to understand the main stages of anger and particularly gain an understanding of the psychological processes, such as that it takes approximately 90 minutes for the body to get back to normal after an angry outburst

- for students to have the opportunity to design personal anger models and reflect upon their own skills in this area.

At the outset, it is vital that the facilitator highlights that anger is a normal and important emotion. It is entirely natural and a necessary part of being a human being. It is the way in which we show and deal with anger that is what tends to cause the most difficulties and problems for us. Anger can be described to students as a flight or fight response to stresses and a secondary emotion that generally occurs from other feelings such as fear or jealousy. It is important that we all recognise our own personal triggers to anger and that we can identify effective ways of managing anger so that it can become a useful tool as opposed to a destructive weapon.

Activity sheet - Brainstorm

Students can work in pairs on this activity that asks them to identify their own personal triggers to anger. For example:

- people putting me down

- people being racist

- when I can't understand the work

- when someone says I am fat

- when I can't get my own way

- when people try to pick a fight with me

- when the teacher doesn't help me.

Students are then asked to identify how many of their triggers are the same as that of their partners and how many are different, alongside reflecting upon the reasons why this may or may not be the case. For example, do most people tend to get angry when they have been humiliated in public? Why would this be the case? This can then enable each pair to consider ten things that they think would make everybody angry. Ideas can then be fed back with the facilitator leading the discussion and recording ideas. This latter part of the activity is important because it emphasises the fact that anger is a normal emotion, and common to all people. There are some situations and events that would cause most people to experience a loss of control and some level of discomfort. It should to be highlighted that anger is part of the fight response to perceived threats and that generally there are functions to anger which are common to all of us, such as a response to frustration, a way of getting what we want or a release of pent up emotions.

Activity sheet - My Anger Model

It is often very useful for both students and adults to have some visual image of the way in which their anger works specifically for them. This may involve recording a list of personal danger words, for example 'fireworks', 'volcano', 'red hot' and 'sparking', alongside drawing what the anger might look like or feel like. Some students may consider the image of a boiling kettle to best reflect their own feelings of pent up anger and frustration while others may feel the image of a volcano erupting is more consistent with the way in which they experience this uncomfortable feeling. The worksheet provides a framework in which to record these ideas.

Activity sheet - Quick Quiz

This final activity requires students to consider a range of 'anger blockers' or 'anger management strategies' that they may or may not make use of. It is helpful for the facilitator to discuss each of the strategies listed and to ensure that students have some clear idea as to what each involves and when or where they may make use of them prior to the students completing the quiz. It would also become apparent that many of these strategies are also effective for stress management and this may allow for some discussion as to the link between stressful situations and the management of angry feelings. Students are asked to identify which of the following they make use of frequently, sometimes or never:

▸ listening to music	▸ humorous thoughts
▸ counting to 10, 20, 30	▸ thinking positive
▸ deep breathing	▸ self-talk
▸ relaxation	▸ going somewhere else
▸ walking away	▸ exercising
▸ ignoring the cause	▸ using a catch phrase
▸ traffic lights	▸ hiding behind an imaginary shield.

Plenary

The facilitator can make use of the whiteboard in order to record students' responses to the activities undertaken in this session. It would be helpful to identify the person's specific nature of both stress and anger while also acknowledging situations and problems that may be common to us all and induce the same level or type of angry response. It is important to be clear that anger can be:

- an emotion
- a loss of control
- an expression of extreme displeasure
- dangerous
- attention seeking
- negative
- dysfunctional
- habit forming

While also being something to build on and something to acknowledge on a frequent basis in order to maintain mental health. If we do not acknowledge and learn how to effectively cope with our anger then we are more at risk of developing hurtful disruptive behaviours which negatively affect both us and those within our learning and social context. Students can focus on their own strategies and perhaps share these at the end of the plenary, identifying those that seem to be most effective for each of the individuals concerned in the group.

Games Activity - Team Bridge

Health and Safety Disclaimer - this activity has the potential to be quite dangerous as there is a lot of trust required between the students when they are in quite precarious positions. We would advise constant vigilance when playing this game, and maybe the use of safety equipment such as helmets and a crash mat.

This activity requires students to construct a bridge and reinforces the notion of co-operation, empathy and the management of personal emotions and responses. This is a problem solving, practical task that demands both co-operation and perseverance. Students are provided with two poles of approximately 3m in length, one pole of approximately 2m in length, three short pieces of rope to leash the poles and one very long rope. Their task is to pass each member of their team over a 'river' without drowning. One member of the team should stand on the other side of the river to act as a 'friendly passer by' and help the team when their structure is ready to be used.

Students are required to build a structure using the poles and short ropes and cross the 'river'. Lashing the poles into a triangle and tying the middle of the long rope at the top can solve the problem. The pupils can then stand on the lower pole having dropped it into the centre of the 'river', and the triangle can be pushed and controlled with the rope over the 'river'. The rope can be used to return the triangle to the first side for the next student. Co-operation is essential.

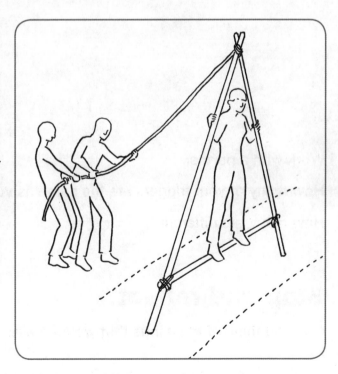

Brainstorm

What are my anger triggers?

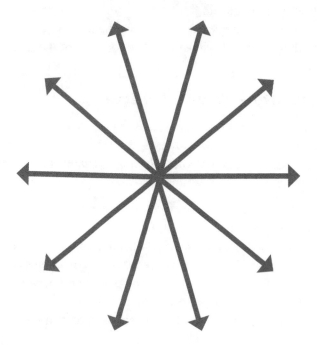

Work with a partner.

How many of your triggers are the same as your partner's?

How many are different?

Stop and reflect.

Can you think of ten things that would make anybody angry?

Anger triggers

How many are the same as your partner?

How many are different?

Ten things we think would make everyone angry.

1

2

3

4

5

6

7

8

9

10

My Anger Model

Quick Quiz

Which anger blockers or anger management strategies do you use?

	Often	Sometimes	Never
Listening to music			
Counting to 10/20/30			
Deep breathing			
Relaxation			
Walking away			
Ignore the situation			
Traffic lights			
Humorous thinking			
Thinking positive			
Self talk			
Go somewhere else			
Exercise			
Using a catchphrase			
Hiding behind an imaginary shield			
Talking it through with a friend			

Session 5
Managing Anger - Part Two

Aims of the session

The facilitator can reinforce aims for the session by use of the whiteboard. The aims can be outlined with students at the very start of the session and opportunities given for further clarification and explanation of specific points. The aims to be recorded are as follows:

▶ for students to further clarify personal triggers to anger

▶ for students to learn about a range of anger blockers and anger management strategies

▶ for students to identify personal anger management strategies and the ways in which they may make use of these in the future

▶ to enable students to distinguish further between positive and negative responses to anger

▶ for students to be able to co-operate in identifying positive and negative behaviours and outcomes and to further support each other in the development of those skills.

Initially, it is helpful for the facilitator to revise and summarise concepts covered in the previous session and to focus upon the range of anger management spoilers and strategies considered to date. It is helpful to have students' anger models on display and to encourage students to explain these to each other while also identifying three anger blockers or strategies which they currently make use of.

Activity sheet - Effective Anger

Provide the students with the activity sheet. This can be photocopied on to card (A4 size). They are then required to cut out a series of eight smaller cards from this sheet and sort each of the statements into two lists. The two lists are the 'do's and don'ts' for effectively managing anger. The statements are as follows:

▶ calm down before you act

▶ put down the other person

▶ be aggressive and confrontational

▶ make the problem bigger than it is

▶ show that you value the other person's feelings even if you don't feel the same

▶ explain your feelings clearly

▶ blame the person you're angry with

▶ suggest another way that it could have been done differently.

Students should work in pairs to complete this activity so as to engender discussion and allow or encourage students to express their views and ideas. Students may wish to feedback to the group as a whole once this activity is completed and the facilitator can reinforce the strategies that would lead to effective anger.

Activity sheet - Effective Anger (2)

Students are then required to write their own two lists of do's and don'ts in order to manage anger most effectively and to then cut these out, jumble them up and ask a partner to re-arrange them or re-arrange them themselves into the two appropriate lists. It is important for the facilitator to emphasise that discussing how we cope with difficult situations and anger and the best ways of doing this is an extremely important strategy in itself. It promotes both self reflection and peer support and these are the two main aims of many of these sessions.

Activity sheet - Problem Cards

This notion of peer support and reflective discussion is reinforced in this activity that requires students to consider a range of anger problems that may be typical situations that they would encounter during the school day. They are then asked to work in pairs or smaller groups to act out both a positive and negative response to each of these situations. This role-play activity will usually involve a simple discussion in which students are encouraged to make use of appropriate vocabulary in order to formulate a positive response to each of the situations. However, the time allowed for this session may not be adequate for students to consider each of the situations and if so it is better to read through them and choose two or three for developing a role-play. The problems identified are as follows:

- you've got loads of extra homework and you feel that this is unfair.
- someone keeps giving you dirty looks for no reason.
- someone has made a nasty comment about your mum.
- you have been fouled in the football match.
- someone is bullying your best friend because she is black.
- you've been blamed for something you didn't do.
- the teacher makes you read out loud in class and you can't read well enough.
- the teacher won't listen to your side of the story.
- you can't understand the work and you feel stupid.
- your mum won't let you go out with your mates because your room is a mess.
- your mum shouts at you for getting up late.
- someone is rude and mouthy to you for no reason.
- people laugh at the way you look or dress.
- someone has told a lie about you.
- you can't get something to work.
- friends leave you out and don't invite you to parties.

This may not be an easy activity for some students and it might be helpful for the facilitator to provide an example. If he has access to another adult or particularly confident member of the group, an example could be constructed prior to the start of the session and acted out at this point. One that we have found particularly helpful (and funny) in the past is

'Your mum shouts at you for getting up late'. It can be quite entertaining for students to watch the teacher taking on the role of the student who gets shouted at and responds in a negative way by shouting back. The facilitator can then display a more positive response in the second scene by not shouting back, getting up as fast as possible and then apologising for causing mum such a level of distress so early in the morning!

The central notion here is that the way in which we respond and behave can actually make a considerable difference to the outcome of each of the situations. The notion of stopping and thinking and thinking before acting is extremely important and it is helpful to reinforce the idea that making use of a stepped approach to problem solving, for example the traffic light or self talk method may be useful for all students to develop in the coming weeks.

Games Activity - The Spider's Web

Students are required to work in small groups in order to complete this activity. The idea is to construct a web between two poles or two trees (if you have access) using string, rope or, best, elastic. Make all lower spaces too small for some students to pass through. The task that students have to complete is to pass each of the team members through the web without touching it. If a team member touches, all must start again. If this is not achieved on a first, second or third go, students are asked to try again and the facilitator can provide hints, such as bigger gaps, higher up, allow for people to be passed through by the team. Co-operation is essential, as students will have to lift each other through, probably in the order of light, heavier, lightest to succeed.

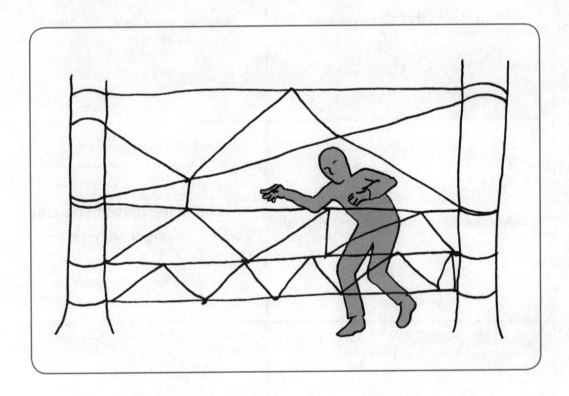

Effective Anger

Cut out and sort these statements into two lists - a list of do's and don'ts for effectively managing anger.

Calm down before you act.	Show that you value the other person's feelings, even if you don't feel the same.
Put down the other person.	Explain your feelings clearly.
Be aggressive and confrontational.	Blame the person you are angry with.
Make the problem bigger than it is.	Suggest another way of how it could have been done differently.

Effective Anger (2)

Add your own do's and don'ts then cut them out and sort with the others!

Write your own 'do' here.	Write your own 'don't' here.
Write your own 'do' here.	Write your own 'don't' here.
Write your own 'do' here.	Write your own 'don't' here.
Write your own 'do' here.	Write your own 'don't' here.

Problem Cards

You got loads of extra homework and you feel that is unfair.	Someone keeps giving you dirty looks for no reason.
Someone has made a nasty comment about your mum.	You have been fouled in the football match.
You have been blamed for something you didn't do.	Someone is bullying your best friend because she's black.
The teacher makes you read out loud in class and you can't read well enough.	The teacher won't listen to your side of the story.
Your mum won't let you go out with your mates because your room's a mess.	You can't understand the work and you feel stupid.

Problem Cards

Your mum shouts at you for getting up late.	Someone is rude and mouthy to you for no reason.
Someone has told a lie about you.	People laugh at you for the way you look or dress.
You can't get something to work.	Friends leave you out and don't invite you to parties.

Session 6

Assertiveness

Aims of the session

The facilitator can record these on a whiteboard prior to the start of the session to act as a prompt for the initial group discussion. The main aims can be identified or recorded as follows:

- for students to understand the distinction between assertiveness, passive and aggressive responses.

- for students to understand the concept of obtaining the best possible outcome by assertive responses to difficult situations

- for students to identify assertive, passive and aggressive responses to a range of problem situations

- for students to further self reflect and analyse their own skills in this area, alongside setting an individual target for improving their use and practice of assertive strategies.

Initially, it is helpful for the facilitator to provide a mini role-play in order to clarify the distinctions for students in the group. For example, ask for a pencil using assertive body language and voice, passive body language and voice and aggressive body language and voice and to ask the group of students to distinguish between each of the requests. It may also be helpful as part of this introduction to ask students to make a request in each of these three ways in order to further reinforce the distinction and make it real for each of them.

Activity sheet - Understanding the Distinctions

This activity asks students to draw three mini self-portraits - an assertive self- portrait, a passive self-portrait and an aggressive self-portrait. These can be done in cartoon style. If the facilitator has copious resources, such as a digital camera, it is a fun activity to make use of this in order to record students' faces in each of these three classifications. The students are then asked to identify what they did and said when they felt assertive, passive and aggressive and this will demand some self reflection and recalling of past events. For example, a student may say, "When I was aggressive I shouted and swore at my mum, I thumped the table, stormed out and banged the door. When I was passive I looked down at my feet and didn't maintain eye contact, I mumbled under my breath, I was unable to say what I wanted. When I was assertive I used an I statement asking for what I wanted, I said how I felt, I kept my voice calm and didn't shout, I stood tall and looked them in the eye."

Activity sheet - Situation Cards

This is a discussion activity in which students are asked to consider eight different problem situations and to then plan out what they would think, say and do in order to achieve the best possible outcome in each of these situations. Should students wish to record their ideas in note form, they could make use of a flip-chart. However, in our experience it has been easier for most of the students in our groups to discuss each of the situations in order to then formulate a joint plan and feed this back to the group as a whole. It is helpful once students have completed the activity, for each small group or pair to feedback on one of the particular problem situations and to identify thoughts, words and actions that may achieve a better outcome for the individual concerned.

Activity sheet - Self-assessment Quiz

In this activity students are asked to reflect on an individual basis, looking at a range of statements and identifying themselves against each statement on a scale of 1 - 10 (1 = hardly ever, 5 = sometimes, 10 = always). Students are asked to mark a point on each of the scales. It will be important to support those students whose literacy skills are under-developed and this will be left to the discretion of the facilitator. Statements are as follows:

- ▸ You generally listen properly to what other people are saying to you.
- ▸ You are honest about what you think and feel to others.
- ▸ You are honest with yourself about your thoughts and feelings.
- ▸ You are sensitive towards other people and can understand how they are feeling.
- ▸ You can ask for what you want.
- ▸ You can take responsibility for your behaviour and the outcomes of your behaviour.
- ▸ You can take responsibility for your choices.
- ▸ You don't rely on other people praising you and thinking you are good.
- ▸ You respect yourself.
- ▸ You respect others.
- ▸ You know that you have rights and so do other people.
- ▸ You are a 'hard' person.
- ▸ You are verbally abusive to others.
- ▸ You are physically abusive to others.
- ▸ You make other people feel upset or unhappy.
- ▸ You always have to win even if others get hurt in the process.
- ▸ You put others down.
- ▸ You force other people to do things that they don't want to do.

Some of these are quite difficult statements for students to have to address. However, it needs to be emphasised that this kind of self reflection demands a level of honesty that really needs to be maintained and further fostered if students are to indeed achieve a better outcome for themselves and learn how to change and modify their own behaviours. The final part of the activity involves students in identifying where their lowest and highest scores were and to set themselves three specific targets in order to further improve their assertive skills. The students are also required to identify a date on which they will review their particular target (via the tutorial process).

Plenary

The facilitator can make use of the whiteboard to elicit or record students' responses as to the usefulness or otherwise of the activities in this session. It is important to reinforce the distinction between assertive, passive and aggressive responses and the ways in which we think, what we say and how we act in certain ways, for example, aggressive behaviours usually result in aggressive responses and no win situations. It is helpful to focus on reinforcing specific vocabulary used and ensuring that students have understood it, for example, passive, aggressive, assertive, analyse best possible outcome, body language, consequences, empathy, self reflection and sensitivity.

Games Activity - Waterproof Shelter

Each group will need some canes, a plastic dustsheet and a limited amount of string. The aim is for them to build a waterproof shelter because a hurricane is on its way! After a pre-set time the team must climb inside their shelter and, if available, a hose can then start for so many minutes. This activity will need to take place outside of the classroom context and adequate time and resources need to be made available to students in order to ensure that this is a stress free, fun and truly social activity.

Once students have completed the activity they can reflect upon it via the usual Circle Time approach, focusing on the following questions:

▶ How did we feel about this activity initially?

▶ What kinds of problems did we think might occur?

▶ What problems actually materialised?

▶ How did we deal with these difficulties?

▶ Could we have dealt with them more effectively?

▶ How will we deal with them better next time?

▶ What do we think we learnt from this activity?

Understanding the Distinctions

Assertive self-portrait	Response - what do you say and do?
	1
	2
	3

Passive self-portrait	Response - what do you say and do?
	1
	2
	3

Aggressive self-portrait	Response - what do you say and do?
	1
	2
	3

Situation Cards

Work out an assertive response to each of these situations. Plan what you would think, say and do in order to achieve the best possible outcome.

You've been asked to go to a party and you know that your ex-girlfriend/boyfriend will be there. She still wants to go out with you and keeps on chasing you. It is getting on your nerves and you wish that you could stop it happening.	Your mum is having some problems with her boyfriend and seems to spend all her time trying to sort them out. She doesn't seem to have any time for you and you feel left out.
Every lunchtime the students in your form take turns to play pool in the hall. The teachers say who can have a go and you are feeling upset and angry because they haven't picked you.	Someone in your class keeps on cussing you about your clothes and says that they are from the charity shop. Your mum hasn't got a lot of money and it's the best you can do. It's making you feel miserable.
Your dad keeps saying that he can't understand why you're not as clever or as well behaved as your elder sister. He says you are a bit of a mug and will never make anything of yourself. You feel hurt as you know you're trying your best.	One of the older boys in the school keeps asking you for money. He says it's for protection but you know he just wants to buy himself cigarettes. You feel a bit nervous about this.
You have been given a detention for something and you know that you didn't do it. The teacher concerned doesn't seem to want to listen to you.	Your mum keeps saying that your schoolwork is not good enough and that she thinks you're a bit stupid. You know that she's sort of joking but you feel angry and upset because you really are trying as hard as you can.

Self-assessment Quiz (1)

Look at the following statements. Be honest! Rate yourself against each statement on a scale of 1 to 10.

(1= hardly ever   5=sometimes   10=always)

Put your mark on each line.

You generally listen properly to what other people are saying to you.

```
1     2     3     4     5     6     7     8     9     10
|llllllllll|llllllllll|llllllllll|llllllllll|llllllllll|llllllllll|llllllllll|llllllllll|llllllllll|
```

You are honest about what you think and feel to others.

```
1     2     3     4     5     6     7     8     9     10
|llllllllll|llllllllll|llllllllll|llllllllll|llllllllll|llllllllll|llllllllll|llllllllll|llllllllll|
```

You are honest with yourself about your thoughts and feelings.

```
1     2     3     4     5     6     7     8     9     10
|llllllllll|llllllllll|llllllllll|llllllllll|llllllllll|llllllllll|llllllllll|llllllllll|llllllllll|
```

You are sensitive towards other people and can understand how they are feeling.

```
1     2     3     4     5     6     7     8     9     10
|llllllllll|llllllllll|llllllllll|llllllllll|llllllllll|llllllllll|llllllllll|llllllllll|llllllllll|
```

You can ask for what you want.

```
1     2     3     4     5     6     7     8     9     10
|llllllllll|llllllllll|llllllllll|llllllllll|llllllllll|llllllllll|llllllllll|llllllllll|llllllllll|
```

You can take responsibility for your behaviour and the outcomes of your behaviour.

```
1     2     3     4     5     6     7     8     9     10
|llllllllll|llllllllll|llllllllll|llllllllll|llllllllll|llllllllll|llllllllll|llllllllll|llllllllll|
```

Self-assessment Quiz (2)

You take responsibility for your choices.

1   2   3   4   5   6   7   8   9   10

You don't rely on other people praising you and thinking you're good.

1   2   3   4   5   6   7   8   9   10

You respect yourself.

1   2   3   4   5   6   7   8   9   10

You respect others.

1   2   3   4   5   6   7   8   9   10

You know that you have rights and so do other people.

1   2   3   4   5   6   7   8   9   10

You are a 'hard' person.

1   2   3   4   5   6   7   8   9   10

You are verbally abusive to others.

1   2   3   4   5   6   7   8   9   10

Self-assessment Quiz (3)

You are physically abusive to others.

1   2   3   4   5   6   7   8   9   10

You make other people feel upset or unhappy.

1   2   3   4   5   6   7   8   9   10

You always have to win even if others get hurt in the process.

1   2   3   4   5   6   7   8   9   10

You put others down.

1   2   3   4   5   6   7   8   9   10

You force other people to do things that they don't want to do.

1   2   3   4   5   6   7   8   9   10

Self-assessment Quiz

Stop, think and reflect!

▶ Where are your highest scores?

▶ Where are your lowest scores?

▶ Do you think that you need to become more assertive?

[ ] Yes   [ ] No

If so, think of three things that you can do in order to achieve this goal. Set your targets and go for it!

Target 1	
Target 2	
Target 3	

I will review these targets on (tutorial)

Signed _____ date _____

Session 7
Stress

Aims of the session

The facilitator can record the aims of the session on the whiteboard prior to the start of the session. This will allow students to discuss each aim in turn with the facilitator and to clarify any definitions or concerns that they may have. This also provides a framework by which the facilitator can introduce this notion of stress and the importance of maintaining and promoting mental health. The aims are as follows:

▶ for students to understand the nature of stress and its main impact upon physical and mental wellbeing

▶ for students to gain a further insight into their own stresses or stress levels and the ways in which they do not or do currently cope with these

▶ for students to understand how the stress is person specific

▶ to develop effective ways of coping with personal stresses alongside understanding basic stress management strategies

▶ to encourage students to adopt a healthy lifestyle and approach in order to achieve a more stress free existence.

It is helpful for the facilitator to initially elicit students' own definitions of stress and to perhaps devise a group definition on which all participants can find some agreement or identify with. A main aim of this session will be to reinforce the fact that stress is, indeed, person specific and something that needs to be seriously acknowledged and addressed in order to enable each individual to reach his or her full potential in both the social and learning context.

Activity sheet - Brainstorm

This activity sheet encourages students to think, reflect and then discuss notions of stress and the causes of stress. They can make use of this brainstorming sheet to record their ideas if they are working individually or as part of a group. However, as indicated in the aims of the session, it may be more helpful for all students to brainstorm as a whole class or group activity. In this case, the facilitator can enlarge the brainstorming sheet to A3 size and utilise this as a means of recording the group's ideas. The second part of the activity asks the students to then rank the stresses that they have recorded in order of severity. They may do this on individual pieces of paper, that is, writing down all the stresses on one piece of paper and then organising them into rank order. Alternatively, they may wish to write a list and number each one of the stressors in rank order. This activity can be undertaken either individually or in pairs and then students can feedback their rankings to the rest of the group and the facilitator can identify any similarities or differences. The main purpose here is to highlight the fact that stress is person specific but that there are certain situations, for example, a bereavement, moving house, divorce, starting a new school or exams that may cause some level of stress to most people. It is important to acknowledge that some so called stressful situations could be regarded as fun or exciting activities for others, such as riding on a big dipper, taking a test or talking or performing in front of a large group of people. It is important for each member of the group to acknowledge these differences and to understand the importance of respecting them.

Activity sheet - Personal Stress Profile

This is an individual activity that aims to identify students' current stress levels and any significant stress symptoms that they may currently have. The ultimate aim is to attempt to identify areas that need to be sorted out quickly in order to ensure that students can cope effectively in most contexts. Students are asked to tick one of five boxes against a range of statements. For example, they are required to ask themselves: Do you get moody and upset (a) all of the time (b) most of time (c) sometimes (d) hardly ever (e) never? Those students who tick the first two boxes (all of the time or most of the time) for the majority of statements in the quiz may be considered to be experiencing an inappropriate level of stress at the moment. It may be that additional one-to-one time needs to be allocated to such students in order to problem solve their current dilemmas. Students are finally asked to discuss with a partner their three most significant stress symptoms and to attempt to identify what may or may not be the causes of these symptoms. This may be a tricky activity for some students and the facilitator will need to be vigilant in observing students' responses and ensuring that students have the option to withdraw from the latter part of the activity if they so desire.

Activity sheet - Stress Busters

This activity sheet details a range of stress busters which students may or may not currently make use of.

Students can do this activity in pairs. They can discuss each of the strategies and to then colour code them according to the following criteria: red = those that you know you would never use; orange = those that you might use in the future and green = those that you use now. The facilitator can highlight certain stress management strategies that are generally agreed to help alleviate stress in most people. For example, having a healthy diet, getting enough sleep, physical exercise and prioritising. It may be helpful to discuss a relaxation script and students could always construct their own relaxation scripts as a follow on activity at a later date if they feel that this would be useful to them.

The final part of this activity asks students to identify any personal strategies that they may be currently using which are not recorded on this sheet. They are asked to identify one new strategy for themselves and to have a go at using it over the next week or so, or whenever they feel stressed or experience too much stress in school or out of school.

Plenary

The facilitator may make use of the whiteboard to record students' views as to how useful or otherwise this session has been. Also, a plenary brainstorming sheet has been provided in order to clarify the facts about stress. The facilitator may wish to enlarge this to A3 or to present each of these on the whiteboard to elicit students' views. This can be done as a group activity or students may wish to do this on an individual or paired basis prior to feeding back to the group. Students are required to work through a list of stress facts and colour code each statement: red being for false and green being for true. The plenary context should allow for any discussion or clarification of specific points. For example,

'Some stress can be managed while other stress can be eliminated,' can appear to be a tricky concept initially. However, after further analysis and discussion students may be able to understand that the stress of going to work and earning enough money to pay bills cannot be eliminated for most people but it can be managed by a range of other strategies and factors.

Games Activity - Escape Tools

For this activity each student is provided with a worksheet. They are required to draw five escape tools on a numbered grid and then to take it in turns to call out any grid reference in order to search for an opponent's tools. This is a paired activity. Students are required to put a cross on a square when they call out the particular reference so that they know it has been searched. If a square is searched and a tool is found then this must be declared and an extra go allocated to the opponent. The player who has all their tools found first is the one who ultimately loses the game. This activity reinforces social and emotional skills and particularly emphasises the importance of co-operation, turn taking and empathy. Also, students are required to be absolutely honest and display some level of trust towards one another when playing this game.

Once students have completed the activity they can reflect upon it via the usual Circle Time approach, focusing on the following questions:

- ▶ How did we feel about this activity initially?
- ▶ What kinds of problems did we think would occur?
- ▶ What problems actually materialised?
- ▶ How did we deal with these difficulties?
- ▶ Could we have dealt with them more effectively?
- ▶ How will we deal with them better next time?
- ▶ What do we think we learnt from this activity?

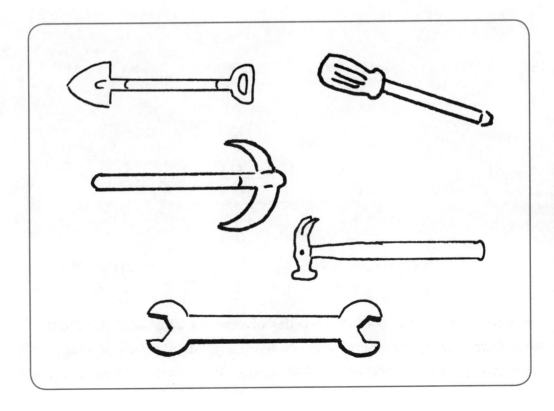

Brainstorm

Think and discuss! What is stress and what causes stress?

Record your ideas on the Brainstorming sheet.

What is stress?

What makes us feel stressed?

Now rank these stressors in the order of severity. Start with the most significant stressor and end with the least significant stressor. Then compare your list with others in the group. Do you agree? If not, why not?

Personal Stress Profile

Signed _____ date _____

Ask yourself! Do you ...	All the time	Most of the time	Some-times	Hardly ever	Never
Get moody and upset?					
Get headaches and migraines?					
Find it difficult to sleep?					
Find it difficult to focus/concentrate?					
Get irritated about minor things?					
Feel anxious/nervous?					
Think things are your fault?					
Feel tired?					
Feel physically sick and wound up?					
Eat too much?					
Not feel like eating?					
Get annoyed with people?					
Think things are pointless?					
Get very angry?					
Feel that you just can't cope?					
Lack confidence?					
Feel alone or lonely?					
Feel worthless?					

Personal Stress Profile

Signed _____   date _____

Ask yourself! Do you ...	All the time	Most of the time	Some-times	Hardly ever	Never
Feel others put you down?					
Keep away from or stop seeing your friends?					
Smoke or drink too much?					
Keep your problems a secret?					
Argue with friends or family?					
Feel tearful?					
Find it hard to make a decision?					
Feel dependant upon drugs?					
Have nightmares or bad dreams?					
Forget things?					
Feel sad?					
Get aches and pains in your muscles?					
Bite your nails?					
Feel yourself clenching your fists?					

How many times have you ticked the first two columns?

Identify the three most significant stress symptoms that you currently have:

1 _____   2 _____   3 _____

Stop and discuss - can you identify the causes of these symptoms? Talk it through with a friend or with your tutor.

Stress Busters

Look at the stress busters and try to identify:

a - those that you know you would never use   (colour red)

b - those you might use in the future   (colour orange)

c - those that you use now   (colour green)

Talk through the problem with a friend.	Use a relaxation script.	Keep to a healthy diet.
Treat yourself to something special or spoil yourself.	Go for a sleep or rest.	Reduce or stop smoking and drinking.
Use a problem solving strategy i.e. make a stepped plan and stick to it.	Use yoga.	Turn the negatives into positives - talk it up!
Get sporty - do physical exercise.	Meditate.	Be assertive and say how you feel.
Listen to calming music.	Take time out and be quiet.	Prioritise the things you have to do and plan your day.

Are there any stress management strategies you use that aren't recorded above? If so, what are they?

Try to identify a new strategy and have a go at using it next time you feel stressed or experience too much stress.

True or False?

What do we know about stress? Is it true or false?

Can we agree? Work through the following STRESS FACTS and colour code each statement. Red = false, green = true

Stress is different for every individual.	Being unfit causes more stress and doing exercise can help you cope better.
Not keeping a balance between work and play can cause stress.	Talking and sharing your feelings can help to solve stress related problems.
Learning to relax can help to reduce stress.	Death or loss causes everyone involved stress.
Family fights or rows cause stress.	Exams cause stress but being organised and planning ahead can reduce this.
Being bullied is a stressor for most students in school.	Too much work causes stress.
Not having enough money makes you stressed.	People can get physical symptoms when they get stressed.
Stress is when you can't cope and feel insecure or helpless.	Solving problems by using step-by-step plans can help reduce stress.
Being organised is a good stress management strategy.	Acting aggressively can increase stress and make stressful situations worse.
Being healthy can reduce stress.	Some stress can be managed whilst other stress can be eliminated.

Escape Tools

1. Draw the five escape tools anywhere on the grid using the number of squares shown.

2. Take it in turns to call out any grid reference to search for your opponent's tools.

3. Put a cross on any square when you call it out so you know it has been searched.

4. If a square is searched and it has a tool in it must be declared and an extra go is allowed.

5. The player who has all their tools found first loses the game.

	1	2	3	4	5	6	7	8	9	10
A										
B										
C										
D										
E										
F										
G										
H										
I										
J										

Spade 3 squares

Pickaxe 2 squares

Screwdriver 2 squares

Hammer 3 squares

Spanner 4 squares

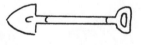

Session 8
Self-esteem - Part One

Aims of the session

The facilitator can record the aims of the session on the whiteboard or flip-chart prior to the start to facilitate group discussion and encourage students to question and articulate the concepts introduced. The main aims of the session are as follows:

▸ for students to understand the concept of self-esteem and how this affects both behaviour and achievement

▸ for students to complete a self-assessment and to clarify their own current levels of self-esteem and identify any areas that they would like to change or improve upon

▸ for students to understand how negative comments and feelings can affect levels of self-esteem

▸ for students to identify strategies of positive thinking which helped to break the negative self-esteem cycle

▸ for students to articulate and celebrate their own positive points, for example attitudes, behaviours, skills or appearance.

It is initially helpful for the facilitator to work with students in identifying an agreed definition as to the nature and properties of self-esteem. Using a thesaurus or dictionary will aid this process initially and these ideas can be recorded on the flip-chart. It is important for students to understand how low levels of self-esteem can be reinforced and how breaking out of the cycle of low self-esteem is an option for each and every individual.

Activity sheet - Self-esteem - An Individual Assessment Profile

Students are required to complete the self-esteem individual assessment profile that aims to identify their current levels of self-esteem. It is important that students are encouraged to think carefully and to be honest about each of the statements. It may also be helpful to allocate an additional peer or adult support for certain students if literacy is not an area of strength and they find the statements too difficult to read and understand. Once students have totalled their ratings on each of the three parts of the quiz, they can then ascertain how well they have done or how good their self-esteem is by referring to the final Summary Sheet.

The important fact here is to reinforce the notion of the possibility of change and of creating a more positive set of responses and behaviours.

Activity sheet - Negatives and Positives

This activity aims to reinforce the notion that negative thinking is the enemy of good self-esteem. Students need to be made aware that talking oneself down and being continually negative on a daily basis only reinforces low levels of self-esteem and doesn't help us to move forwards. It is important to highlight that most of us tend to make use of negative statements quite frequently throughout each day. It is a trap that is very, very easy to fall into and not a particularly helpful one. What we need to be able to do is to turn our negative thoughts and feelings into positive ones by articulating or reframing negative statements in a more positive way. In this activity the students are required to turn the ten negative statements into positives.

It is helpful for the facilitator to demonstrate turning the first statement into a positive so that students can get the general idea. For example, "I am rubbish at maths and I'll never be able to understand it," can be reframed as "I find maths difficult but I know I can get extra help, and if I take it step by step and work methodically I can make my skills improve."

Activity sheet - My Positive Points

It is important for students to be able to identify positive facts about themselves and to have these reinforced on a daily basis to maintain and further develop positive levels of self-esteem. It is helpful to have taken digital photographs of students prior to the start of this session to complete this worksheet. Students are required to identify positive points or aspects about themselves and to record these in the stars around the sheet. They are then asked to take this sheet home, stick it on to the back of their bedroom door, and to look at it every day before they leave the house. The facilitator can acknowledge the fact that some people find it extremely difficult to pay themselves compliments or to acknowledge good things about themselves and that not to do so will reinforce negative levels of self-esteem and behaviours which do not engender change or positive thoughts and feelings.

Plenary

The facilitator can utilise the whiteboard to summarise the main points covered in this session to reinforce the notion that positive self-esteem can be developed through a process of positive thinking, self-talk and peer support. Students are being asked to be both reflective and solution focused in this session and it is helpful to reinforce these concepts and to ensure that students have an appropriate understanding of the following vocabulary: empathy, negative thinking, positive thinking, self-esteem, self-concept, self reflection, peer support and confidence.

Games Activity - Team Chair Relay

Students need to be placed in groups for this activity. Each group will need some chairs but there must be fewer chairs than members of the group. The aim is for team members to move along a route (created by these chairs) without touching the ground. This activity will probably need to take place outside of the classroom context. Adequate time and resources need to be made available to students so as to ensure that this is a fun and truly social activity in which they can further develop social skills and the ability to co-operate effectively as a member of the team.

Finally, once students have completed the activity they can reflect upon it via the usual Circle Time approach, focusing on the following questions:

- How did we feel about this activity initially?

- What kinds of problems did we think would occur?

- What problems actually materialised?

- How did we deal with these difficulties?

- Could we have dealt with them more effectively?

- How will we deal with them better next time?

- What do we think we learnt from this activity?

Self-esteem Individual Assessment Profile

Completed by _____ date _____

Think carefully and be honest!

Tick box A = Never   Tick box B = Sometimes

Tick box C = Often   Tick box D = Always

Part I

	A	B	C	D
Do you think people like you?				
Do you think that you have 'good' friends?				
Do you feel that you have good relationships at home?				
Do you feel confident when you're asked to do something new or different?				
Can you admit it when you've made a mistake?				
Are you OK at most things?				
Do you feel happy about meeting new people or making new friends?				
Do you trust most people?				
Are you able to relax and enjoy yourself?				

PART 1 - Add up your score   A = 1   Total

                                    B = 2

                                    C = 3

                                    D = 4

Self-esteem Individual Assessment Profile

Completed by _____ date _____

Think carefully and be honest!

Tick box A = Never   Tick box B = Sometimes

Tick box C = Often   Tick box D = Always

Part 2

	A	B	C	D
Do you get miserable if other people criticise you?				
Do you feel jealous of other students and their lives?				
Do you worry about what others think of you?				
Do you think you need to impress others by the way you look?				
Do you think that other people don't understand you?				
Do you often feel left out or excluded?				
Do you dislike people (without telling anyone about it?)				
Do you keep your problems a secret?				
Do you try to please people all the time?				
Do you 'put yourself down'?				

PART 2 - Add up your score   A = 4   Total [ ]
                                   B = 3

                                     C = 2

                                     D = 1

Self-esteem Individual Assessment Profile

Completed by _____ date _____

Think carefully and be honest!

Tick box A = Never   Tick box B = Sometimes

Tick box C = Often   Tick box D = Always

Part 3

	A	B	C	D
Do you feel depressed about your life situation?				
Do you feel that you 'miss out' on the chances that others have?				
Do you make excuses for not doing the things you know you'd really like to do?				
Do you feel that your life is hopeless?				
Do you feel that other students have better relationships than you?				
Do you think you have to try and impress others with the way you act and behave at school?				
Do you feel shy or awkward in some situations?				
Do you feel 'fed-up' at the end of each day?				

PART 1 - Add up your score   A = 4   Total
                             B = 3
                             C = 2
                             D = 1

How Did You Do?

Score 28-43

Your self-esteem is low so you need to work on it in order to become a happier and more confident person. You need to start to think more positively and really believe that you can change and start to feel better about yourself.

You can start by making one or two small changes in order to feel better about yourself and change you own self-perception and the way you think others feel about you. Time to go for it!

Score 44-73

You self-esteem is up and down. You need to start to feel more in control and more confident about your coping strategies. It's time for you to build yourself up and put yourself forward a bit more. You now need to identify the things that have made you feel fragile before and to work out how you can begin to sort things out for the best. It's time to clean up and shape up. Go for it!

Score 74-102

Your self-esteem is generally OK but you may still lack confidence in a few areas. These need to be sorted out now so that you can become more confident in yourself and you really start to recognise and make the most of all the opportunities that are out there for you. It's time for you to build on your self-esteem a bit more! Go for it!

Score 103-112

Your self-esteem is fine! You are mainly positive and feel confident about yourself and your life. Set yourself some new or more challenging goals - make them bigger and better. Go on, go for it!

Negatives and Positives

Negative thinking is the enemy of good self-esteem.

Look at the negative statements. Can you change them into positives?

-	**+**
I'm rubbish at maths and I'll never be able to understand it.	
My mum doesn't have any time for me because she's got a new boyfriend.	
I'll never be able to get a boyfriend because I'm too shy.	
I don't have any friends and I feel lonely.	
I won't be able to pass my exams because I haven't done enough work.	
My face is covered in spots and I look odd.	
The English teacher never listens to me because she doesn't like me.	
I'll never get back into mainstream school because the teachers won't let me back.	
There's no point in me going to school because the lessons are rubbish and boring.	
Make one up yourself.	

My Positive Points

Write down ten positive points about yourself in the stars.

Stick a photo of yourself here.

Keep positive. Stick this sheet on the back of your bedroom door and look at it every day before you leave the house.

Session 9

Self-esteem - Part Two

Aims of the session

The facilitator can write the aims on the whiteboard prior to the start of the session in order to facilitate the initial discussion. The main aims of this second self-esteem session are as follows:

- for students to understand the importance of keeping positive and learning to accept positive compliments or feedback from others

- to understand how negative feelings or negative levels of self-esteem mitigate the ability to accept both positive and negative feedback

- for students to provide positive feedback for each other

- for students to further develop empathy and joint problem-solving skills

- for students to identify ways in which they can maintain or further develop their own self-esteem and the self-esteem of others.

Reinforce the notion of self-esteem by referring to definitions agreed in the previous session and then further develop this theme by outlining the main activities to be covered in this session.

Activity sheet - A Golden Scroll

Depending on the size of the group, it is helpful to have identified the student for whom a golden scroll can be completed prior to the start of the session. However, if this is a small group then each student can receive a golden scroll from other members of the group. The idea is for each student to make a positive comment about an individual and to have these recorded on the golden scroll which can then be taken home by the student who is being focused upon. This will help to reinforce self-esteem and to raise students' awareness as to how they can impact on the self-esteem of others by making positive comments and providing positive and empathetic feedback.

Activity sheets - Problem Page

This activity requires students to look at a series of four problems, all of which students may have experienced at one point or another within their lives. Each problem highlights how the individual has low levels of confidence and self-esteem due to a range of different factors and contexts. Students are required to work with a partner and to try to help each of the problem page writers by producing a reply on the problem solver worksheet. They should give what they perceive to be realistic advice as to how each writer can improve their self-esteem. The idea is to be solution focused and to identify practical things that each student can do to solve their particular problem.

This activity aims to reinforce the importance of empathy and the need to provide each other with an adequate level of peer support. It also highlights the fact that having friends and positive relationships is a major influence on our levels of self-esteem.

Activity sheet - Self-esteem Building Targets

This activity reinforces the importance of supporting others and using positive talk and compliments in order to raise self-esteem. However, it is important to point out that accepting compliments is much harder when your level of self-esteem is low and that the most important thing is to ensure that the compliment or positive feedback is entirely sincere and based in reality. For example, it is not healthy or useful to say to someone who is obese, "You're looking really well and you have lost lots of weight," when they clearly haven't. It is more helpful to suggest ways in which they may be able to help themselves and to say how nicely they are presenting themselves or how well they have done their hair or how good their skin looks.

In this activity students are required to identify five ways in which they can help themselves remain positive and build up their own level of self-esteem and five ways in which they can help others. It can be helpful for them to identify people who they would like to help as this will ensure that the activity is based in real life as opposed to fantasy.

Plenary

The facilitator can make use of the whiteboard or flip-chart in order to record students' ideas and responses to the activities undertaken in this session. Ask the question, "What have we learnt about our self-esteem?" This will encourage the reinforcement of key concepts and strategies. It will also allow the students to identify personal targets for maintaining their own levels of self-esteem and for further promoting that of others within their peer group. It is helpful to reinforce some of the vocabulary introduced in this session and to ensure that each student has understood and absorbed the relevant definition. Vocabulary may include the following: compliments, constructive criticism, empathy, motivators, positive reinforcement, praise, problem solving, peer support, self-esteem, self-image, self-concept and self reflection.

Games Activity - The Human Knot

In this activity, students only require adequate space and time. They should be stood in a circle and each student is asked to put his hand in to grasp the right hand of the person opposite. Each student then puts forward their left hand and grasps the left hand of any other individual in the circle apart from the one whose right hand they are currently holding. Finally, without letting go, the team must 'un-knot' themselves into a ring. This activity may need to take place outside of the classroom context depending on the size of the group. This activity aims to promote and reinforce each student's ability to co-operate effectively as a member of the team.

Once students have completed the activity they can reflect upon it via the usual Circle Time approach, focusing on the following questions:

- ▸ How did we feel about this activity initially?
- ▸ What kinds of problems did we think would occur?
- ▸ What problems actually materialised?
- ▸ How did we deal with these difficulties?
- ▸ Could we have dealt with them more effectively?
- ▸ How will we deal with them better next time?
- ▸ What do we think we learnt from this activity?

A Golden Scroll

Positive comments we have made about _____

We hope this helps you to feel good about yourself! Keep reading the scroll especially when you begin to feel down.

Problem Page

Look at the Problem Page letters. Read them carefully.

During the last year my dad has got married again. His new wife is a lot younger than my mum and she is very thin and good-looking. She keeps making comments about how flabby I am and how I look bad in all my clothes. She says that no one will ever fancy me because I look so dowdy and boring. I used to think I was OK but now I'm beginning to feel really bad about myself. Please help.

Yours, Hui Ying

My ears stick out and I've got loads of spots. Other kids keep picking on me because they say I'm ugly. I feel really fed up and down about it. I look at myself in the mirror first thing and I just don't want to leave the house. What can I do?

Yours, Tara

All the other kids in my form have got girlfriends but I can't seem to get one. I think it's because I'm so small and the girls think I'm younger than I am. This is making me feel bad because it's like I'm not part of what is going on outside school. I can't go to parties without a girlfriend and there is no point in going if I can't even get a girl to notice me. What can I do? Can you help?

Yours, Rafiki

In my Maths lessons I find the work really hard. Every time the teacher asks me a question I just don't get it. I think he wants to show me up so I just start shouting. It makes me feel dumb and then I get into more trouble. What can I do?

Yours, Dawud

Now work with a partner and try to help each writer by writing a reply on the 'Problem Solver' activity sheet. Try to give realistic advice to how each writer can improve their self-esteem.

Problem Solver

Use the postcards to write back to each student. Try to give them good advice that will help them to sort out their problem and increase their self-esteem. Discuss and work with a partner.

Dear Tara,

I think you should

_____

_____

_____

_____

_____

To Tara

_____

_____

Dear Hui Ying,

I think you should

_____

_____

_____

_____

_____

To Hui Ying

_____

_____

Problem Solver (2)

Dear Dawud,

I think you should

_____

_____

_____

_____

_____

To Dawud

_____

_____

Dear Rafiki,

I think you should

_____

_____

_____

_____

_____

To Rafiki

_____

_____

Self-esteem Building Targets

How can you build your own self-esteem? How can you help others to feel better about themselves? Complete the chart below.

Say something kind!
Be constructive.
Smile

Five ways I can help myself	Five ways I can help others
1	1
2	2
3	3
4	4
5	5

Don't forget to try these out!

Session 10

Classroom Survival

Aims of the session

As usual the facilitator can record the aims of the session on the whiteboard or flip-chart prior the start of the session. This will, hopefully, provide prompts for the initial introductory discussion and encourage students to question any of the new concepts or ideas introduced. The aims of this session are as follows:

- for students to discuss and identify the qualities of a 'perfect' teacher

- for students to discuss and identify the qualities of a 'perfect' pupil

- to further develop empathy for the teacher, i.e. by putting themselves in the teacher's shoes and considering how they feel when negative events occur in their classroom

- to consider whose responsibility it is to ensure good behaviour in the classroom and to further clarify the responsibilities of both staff and students

- to identify the qualities or strategies that students need to develop in order to successfully survive the classroom context

- for students to be able to reflect honestly upon the current level of their own skills and to formulate realistic targets for themselves in terms of further developing appropriate skills and strategies.

In this session students are presented with the notions of accountability and responsibility. They are particularly encouraged to consider how and when they are responsible for themselves in the classroom and their responsibility towards those who are teaching them. Just as they will hopefully be beginning to empathise with one another, they will also need to develop empathy for those adults in the school or learning context who attempt to support them and aid them in the development of their skills.

Activity sheet - My Ideal Teacher

This activity requires students to identify the main characteristics of a so-called 'ideal teacher', that is, someone who is, in the eyes of the student, a perfect practitioner. They should be able to develop a positive relationship with the student alongside ensuring that real learning takes place. Students are asked to make use of the portrait frame to illustrate this idea and then to record qualities around the outside of the portrait frame. Once each student has completed this activity it is helpful for them to work in pairs or as a group to complete the second part which asks, 'How does the ideal teacher help you to:

- ▸ learn well
- ▸ enjoy the lesson
- ▸ behave well?'

Students are asked to record their ideas on the back of the sheet. However, the facilitator can record these on the whiteboard or flip-chart particularly if there are issues around certain students' literacy skills and ability to record independently. The essential idea within this activity is that of the teacher being in control and being able to ensure learning enjoyment and good behaviour within the classroom context. It is important for students to understand how teachers may or may not be able to do this and to reflect upon the ways in which they may have prevented teachers from doing so in the past.

Activity sheet - The Perfect Pupil

This activity requires students to put themselves in the teacher's shoes; it is a further development of empathy. They are asked to imagine that they are the teacher and to identify the qualities of a so-called perfect pupil. This can lead to some interesting discussion, for example, some students may well think that the ideal pupil in the teacher's eyes is someone who is extremely clever, doesn't talk in class and gets on with their work. It is quite interesting for the facilitator to also complete this activity and to perhaps highlight the fact with the group of students that teachers very often enjoy engaging in conversation with students - they like to hear students' ideas; they don't actually have a problem with students who find the work difficult but simply want them to do their best and show that they are motivated and willing to engage with the activities presented. Once this initial part of the activity has been completed, both the students and the facilitator can compare their ideas and qualities and these can be recorded on the flip-chart or whiteboard as appropriate.

The second part of the activity requires students to reflect on the following questions:

- ▸ Whose responsibility is it to make sure that pupils behave well?
- ▸ Is the teacher totally responsible?
- ▸ Is the pupil totally responsible?
- ▸ What do you think?

Students are asked to record their ideas on the back of the sheet. It may be more appropriate for students to feedback to the facilitator who can act as a scribe, particularly if some students' literacy skills are under developed. These questions do facilitate a great deal of very interesting discussion and reinforce the notions of locus of control, empathy and responsibility. It is important that students understand that both the teacher and the student are probably equally responsible for the behaviour management and learning that takes place within the classroom context. They can begin to understand that true learning demands a partnership approach and that they have a responsibility within that partnership. The idea is to reinforce this notion of joint responsibility.

Activity sheet - Top Tips for surviving in class

Students are required to work on this quiz individually. They are presented with a list of survival strategies and techniques and are asked to reflect upon whether they currently make use of these strategies. Each statement is presented as an 'I can' sentence to reinforce a positive and affirmative approach. For example, 'I can be in the right place at the right time,' 'I can sit in the right place without any fuss,' 'I can listen to the teacher's instructions,' 'I can keep the class rules,' and 'I can work as part of a group.' Students are asked to record three of their own 'I can' statements and then to add the number of ticks on the sheet. Any gaps indicate to each student areas that they may need to develop and provide prompts for setting targets during the subsequent activity.

Activity sheet - How Do I Rate?

The final activity of the session requires students to rate themselves on a scale from 1 - 10 as to how perfect a pupil they think they are. (1 = worst pupil in the world, 5 = okay pupil, 10 = the perfect pupil). It is important that students reflect honestly and consider the perspectives of others, as well as themselves, when making this rating. It is important for students to be very clear that there are things that they can do presently, although some of these skills may not be transferred into contexts as yet. They are asked to list the things that they know they can currently do on the reverse of the sheet, or to feedback verbally to a partner.

The second part of this activity is entitled, 'Set your Targets'. Students are here required to list four things that they need to do in order to move up the scale and then to record these on the second part of the sheet. It would be helpful if students could then make use of these targets during their next tutorial session when they can be reviewed and perhaps incorporated into the weekly plan.

Plenary

The facilitator can act as a scribe for students' ideas and feedback as to how useful they felt this session was. They should reflect upon a series of questions, for example: What have we learnt in this session?

What difference do we think this would make to us?

What difference do we think it may make to others?

What new vocabulary skills or strategies have we learnt to date?

The facilitator can now revise some of the key concepts learnt and ensure that students have an understanding of key vocabulary used, for example locus of control, responsibility, self reflection, accountability, empathy and survival techniques.

Games Activity - Team Desert Island

At the outset, the facilitator needs to set the scene for this activity, asking the students to imagine that they have are on a boat trip and their boat has hit a rock and started to sink. They have no choice but to swim to a nearby desert island.

This activity does not require additional space but does require the facilitator to collect a set of ten items for each group. The items include a compass, a mirror, a scarf, a box of matches, a bottle of water, a kettle, a rope, a roll of sticky tape, a pair of scissors and a sunhat. Students are required to decide which five items they would take with them as they swim from their sinking boat. Which ones are essentials and will make their survival more likely? For example, the mirror might be essential as it could be used for reflecting sunrays to signal to a passing ship for rescue. However the sticky tape would provide no real purpose on a desert island. This activity should promote a great deal of debate and students can be encouraged to justify their choices and to think of a wide range of possible outcomes and scenarios.

The main aim is to encourage students to come to an agreement through a process of co-operation and compromise.

Once students have completed the activity they can reflect upon it via the usual Circle Time, focusing on the following questions:

- How did we feel about this activity initially?

- What kinds of problems did we think would occur?

- What problems actually materialised?

- How did we deal with these difficulties?

- Could we have dealt with them more effectively?

- How will we deal with them better next time?

- What do we think we learnt from this activity?

My Ideal Teacher

What makes a good teacher? Brainstorm your ideas around the portrait.

Draw it!

Stop, think and reflect

How does the ideal teacher help you to:

▶ learn well?

▶ enjoy the lesson?

▶ behave well?

Record your ideas on the back of this sheet.

The Perfect Pupil

What makes a perfect pupil? What would the teacher say? Try to put yourself in the teachers' shoes. Brainstorm your ideas around the portrait.

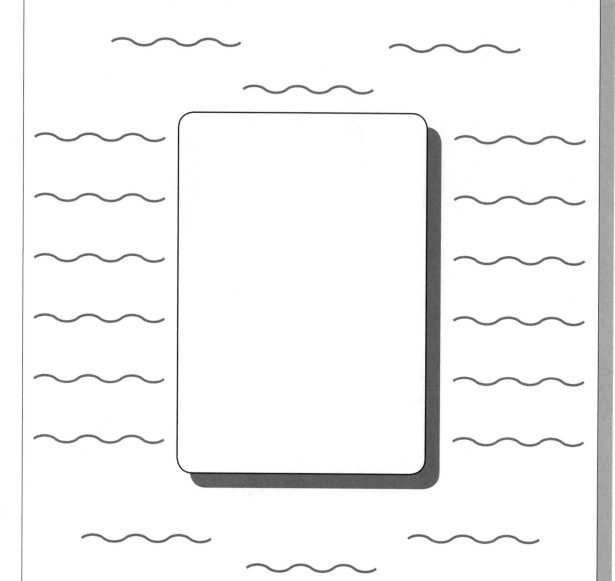

Stop, think and reflect

▶ Whose responsibility is it to make sure that pupils behave well?

▶ Is the teacher totally responsible?

▶ Is the pupil totally responsible?

▶ What do you think?

Record your ideas on the back of this sheet.

Draw it.

Top Tips for surviving in class

Look at the list. Which of these things do you do? Tick against each statement and then add on a few of your own ideas if you can.

I can be in the right place at the right time.	
I can line up properly outside a classroom.	
I can walk sensibly into the classroom.	
I can sit in the right place without any fuss.	
I have the right equipment for each lesson.	
I can listen to the teacher's instructions.	
I can respond appropriately to the teacher in a polite manner.	
I can wait for help if the teacher is busy for one minute	
...two minutes	
...three minutes	
...more.	
I can try something even if I'm not sure how to do it.	
I know the class rules.	
I can keep the class rules.	
I can work as part of a group.	
I can stay in class unless I have permission to leave.	
I can ask politely if I do need to leave the room.	
I can stay in my seat.	
I can write down my homework.	
I can treat the classroom/school property with respect.	
I can clear up when asked.	
I can leave the classroom quietly and sensibly when asked.	
I can	
I can	
I can	

How Do I Rate?

How perfect a pupil are you? Complete the scaling activity. Think carefully and be honest. Make the scale!

1=worst pupil in the world   5=OK pupil   10=the perfect pupil

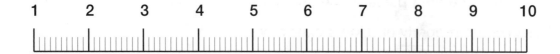

Where are you on the scale?

List the things you know you can do now.

Set your targets

List four things that you need to do in order to move up the scale. Record these as targets below.

	I need to
Target 1	I need to
Target 2	I need to
Target 3	I need to
Target 4	I need to

Have a go! Try to reach your targets. Look back at the end of each week and think about how you have done. Go for it!

Session 11
Developing Empathy

Aims of the session

The facilitator can record the aims of the session on a whiteboard prior to the start of the session and to then use these as a prompt for the introductory discussion. The main aims are as follows:

- for students to understand what is meant by empathy and to be able to distinguish between empathising with others and showing sympathy

- to further develop students' ability to empathise with other pupils' difficult situations via a range of problem solving activities

- for students to understand the importance of how we respond verbally to others and the need to 'stop and think' before speaking

- to reinforce the skills of being a good listener, taking turns, giving positive feedback and reinforcing others' confidence and how this is a two way process

- to understand the importance of developing empathy in order to ensure and maintain positive relationships with others.

The notion of empathy has arisen in the majority of previous sessions and it would be helpful for students to have access to dictionaries or thesauruses to complete the first definitions activity. It is important to emphasise that without developing empathy, it is unlikely that students will be able to sustain and develop positive relationships both in and outside of the school context. It is consequently crucial that they understand the importance of this particular skill in terms of surviving and maintaining mental and emotional wellbeing.

Activity sheet - What is Empathy?

Students can work in pairs or as a whole group to brainstorm their ideas. If the latter option is chosen the facilitator can scribe students' responses on the whiteboard or flip-chart and enlarge the worksheet to A3 size for this purpose.

The second part of this activity requires students to identify the differences between empathy and sympathy. This can be done via discussion in pairs and then fed back to the group as a whole with the facilitator acting as a scribe. This is an extremely important distinction and needs to be made clear at the outset of the session. Empathy does not mean that you feel sorry for somebody, but rather that you can put yourself in his shoes. Imagining feeling like or being somebody else is reinforced in the next activity.

Activity sheet - Put yourself in my shoes

These three sheets provide students with nine scenarios in which individual characters describe a dilemma or problem situation that they currently find themselves in. Students are asked to read through the scenarios and to then identify how each of the characters may feel. Students can be divided into smaller groups or pairs, particularly if some have difficulty with basic literacy skills. They can choose one or two of the scenarios on which to feedback to the rest of the group. It may be interesting to compare notes here, such as, 'Do students come to an agreement as to how a certain individual feels or do they perceive a situation differently?' 'Why would this be the case?' The course facilitator can run through each of the characters in turn asking students to individually feedback their ideas and views in the feedback session. This activity requires students not only to be empathetic but to also be reflective and to analyse the context of each individual's dilemma. They are also being required to utilise an emotional vocabulary and to further develop this particular skill.

Activity sheet - What Would You Say?

This activity focuses on developing an emotional vocabulary and the ability to find the words necessary to empathise with someone else. Students are asked to study a range of statements and to think what they would say in order to show empathy for each of the pupils concerned. They are then required to record their response in each of the speech bubbles. Students with low levels of literacy attainment can be aided in this and members of the group can act as a scribe or the facilitator can fulfil this role as appropriate.

The facilitator can provide an example at the outset of this activity by articulating his own response to one of these statements. For example, "I'm so rubbish at writing. I may as well not even try. I feel so dumb." The response to this may be, "I can understand it's difficult for you and that must make you feel quite bad but you could get some help from Mr or Mrs so-and-so and you could use the computer a bit and some of those games to build up your skills. Don't feel dumb because everyone finds things hard. You just need to accept some help and really try. I'll help you if you like."

Underlining this activity is the notion that students can provide support and help to each other. Showing empathy may not mean just saying nice and helpful words but may also involve nice and helpful actions as well.

Plenary

It is useful for the facilitator to record students' responses to the activities within this session utilising the whiteboard or flip-chart as appropriate. It is important to emphasise the distinction between empathy and sympathy and to ensure that all students have understood both the meaning of this concept and how they can empathise with those around them. The notion that empathy may also involve feelings, words and actions can be reinforced alongside certain key vocabulary as follows:

- ▸ empathy
- ▸ sympathy
- ▸ positive feedback
- ▸ emotional vocabulary
- ▸ active listening
- ▸ problem-solving.

Games Activity - Team Tea Break

In keeping with theme of ESCAPE and survival, students are asked to work together in groups to make a cup of tea with a limited amount of equipment. This activity should take place outdoors where fires are permitted. The main purpose is to build up a sense of peer support and team working alongside reinforcing co-operation and empathy. Students will need some pieces of wood, a pan or pot, some matches or a lighter, tea bags and mugs. Water collection could be made more difficult if this seems appropriate for the groups concerned. This can be achieved by providing only a small cup or a sheet of plastic. The 'winners' will be the group who manage to take a tea break first.

The facilitator should remind the students of group rules and the fact that all of these games activities reinforce the social and emotional skills that they will need in order to function appropriately within the mainstream context.

Once students have completed the activity they can reflect upon it via the usual Circle Time approach, focusing on the following questions:

- ▶ How did we feel about this activity initially?
- ▶ What kinds of problems did we think would occur?
- ▶ What problems actually materialised?
- ▶ How did we deal with these difficulties?
- ▶ Could we have dealt with them more effectively?
- ▶ How will we deal with them better next time?
- ▶ What do we think we learnt from this activity?

What is Empathy?

Stop, think and reflect!

How do we empathise? What does this involve? Record your ideas on the brainstorming chart below. Some people may confuse 'empathy' with 'sympathy.' What do you think the differences are between these two feelings?

Discuss in pairs and feedback to the group.

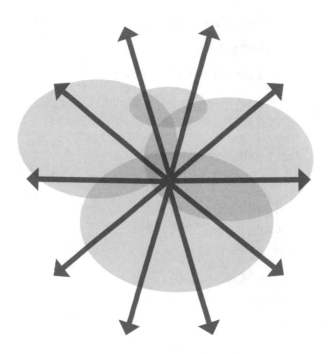

Put yourself in my shoes (1)

Take one or two of the following scenarios. Read through each one carefully and then try to explain to the rest of the group how the character in the scene feels.

Jahi was waiting for the train to come. It was late again and it didn't help that it was pouring with rain and getting colder by the minute. He shivered and pulled his coat around him. Then he saw a group of older boys walking towards him. They were laughing and shouting. He wasn't sure if they were shouting at him but he turned his back just in case.

How do you think Jahi feels?

Mrs. Connors placed all her materials on the front desk. She was very keen to start the lesson as she knew that Year 8 would really enjoy it. She'd got the video camera all set up so that she could film the role-plays and then show these to the class during the second half of the lesson. It had been a lot of work but she felt that it would be worth it. The bell went and Year 8 started to come in. She asked them to sit down. Two boys who were coming in last said, "Get lost, why should we?" Mrs Connors couldn't believe it. She hadn't expected this and she couldn't handle it. She screamed at them both to get out.

How do you think Mrs Connors feels?

Carla saw her mum topple over and fall on to the sofa. She looked dreadful. Her skin was bright pink and blotchy and she stank of alcohol. She lay on the sofa and started singing loudly. Carla walked over to her mum and said, "Come on, go to bed now mum or you'll wake the neighbours and they'll complain again." But Carla's mum just ignored her and then turned round and shouted, "Just go to bed yourself you little idiot."

How do you think Carla feels?

Put yourself in my shoes (2)

Kiran had been going out with Michael for just over two months. She was really crazy about him and she knew all the other girls in her form were jealous because he was good looking and a good laugh. He didn't try to show-off or be macho like most other boys of his age. She was really shocked and her illusions were shattered when she found out that he'd been two-timing her for the last two weeks. She confronted him and he said he didn't see the problem as they weren't married or committed and that she could go out with other boys as well if she wanted to.

How do you think Kiran feels?

Elen had a thyroid problem that meant that she'd put on a lot of weight during the last year. Before she'd been diagnosed with this condition she had been quite slim and felt good about the way she looked. Now she was bigger and less fit she wasn't able to play for the netball team. She'd have to wait for about three months until the drugs started to have an effect. She went to watch last night's netball match but had to leave before the end because other members of the team had started to call her a fat, lazy cow and said she couldn't be bothered to play anymore.

How do you think Elen feels?

Hiroshi's dad had just died of lung cancer. He'd been ill for about a month and during this time he was frequently put on a ventilator so he couldn't communicate with anyone very much. Just before he got really ill, Hiroshi had a big argument with him about school and his behaviour. His dad had been very upset and Hiroshi couldn't cope with it so he'd said, "I wish you'd just hurry up and die."

How do you think Hiroshi feels?

Put yourself in my shoes (3)

Hasad had always been good at sport and prided himself on keeping fit and healthy. He was regularly picked for the school football team and always won the major athletic events every Sports Day. When he moved house and started a new school in September of this year he quickly found out about the sports activities that were going on and when trials for the football team were taking place. He was really keen to play for a new team and to show his new friends what he could do on the pitch. Unfortunately, he didn't make it through the first round of the trials.

How do you think Hasad feels?

Keith's best mate Jez was probably one of the best mates he'd ever had. He was always having a laugh and would always stick up for you if someone started having a go. They had been good friends since the start of Year 7 and were both hoping to go to college together and to do mechanics. Then Jez met a couple of older boys through his big brother and started hanging around with them and doing drugs. He stopped speaking to Keith and didn't want to be around him any more.

How do you think Keith feels?

Mr. Purwall had lived in London since 1955 and was now a grandfather and successful shopkeeper with three shops in his local area. He worked hard and was proud of what he and his family had achieved from virtually nothing. He now worked part-time in one of his shops as he was beginning to feel tired and less able to manage a whole day; this wasn't surprising since he was now 86. He had made a lot of good friends in the community and always enjoyed chatting to his customers. He hadn't been the victim of any abuse until recently when a new family moved into the area. There were three of their boys in particular who regularly shouted abuse at him and yesterday they threatened to torch his shop and called him a Paki.

How do you think Mr Purwall feels?

What Would You Say?

Sometimes it can be quite hard to find the words needed to empathise with someone else. Look at the following statements and try to think what you could say in order to show empathy for each person. Write your response in the speech bubbles.

"I'm so rubbish at writing. I may as well not even try. I feel so dumb!"

"My dad has grounded me for smoking. It's so unfair when he smokes himself."

"I'm so ugly. I feel that I need plastic surgery or I'll never get a girlfriend."

"That teacher has just got it in for me. I keep getting into trouble and it's not my fault. She just wants me out."

"My mum keeps on saying how disappointed she is in me for getting excluded. She says I'm bad, I feel so fed up, it's all useless."

Session 12

Problem-solving - Part One

Aims of this session

The facilitator can record the aims on the flip-chart or whiteboard prior to the start of the session. This list can then be used to facilitate the initial discussion and introduce the concepts to be covered within the session. The aims of the session can be recorded as follows:

▸ for students to reflect upon their own skills in the area of conflict management and to identify both positive and negative behaviours and areas and skills that they might need to develop further

▸ for students to undertake a self reflection activity in order to understand how adopting a stepped approach to problem-solving can be effective and ensure a more positive outcome

▸ to understand the positive results of a conflict and to distinguish between win/win, win/lose, lose/lose outcomes and why we need to aim for a win/win outcome

▸ for students to consider and hopefully adopt a range of strategies to ensure win/win outcomes.

Within this session students will be asked to reflect upon their own skills in this area and to identify ways in which they can develop these further. This will require an honest and analytical approach and students should be encouraged to be both truthful and clear about where they are currently and where they would like to go or be in the future. Being positive, solution focused, assertive, empathetic and not aggressive will usually facilitate the most positive outcomes and it would be helpful to reinforce these facts throughout this session and Session 13 that follows on and reinforces the concepts introduced here.

Activity sheet - Coping with Conflict

This activity requires students to reflect on a series of statements as to how they normally handle a conflict or problem situation. Students are required to tick against the statements that most reflect their current behaviours.

Students are then asked to stop, think and reflect on whether or not their behaviours or responses achieve the best outcomes and to then consider three ways in which they might act differently in order to achieve a better result for themselves. They may wish to conduct this part of the activity in pairs and to then feedback to the group as a whole. The facilitator can decide on which option is most appropriate for the group in question.

It is helpful to reinforce the notions of passive, assertive and aggressive responses to conflict and perhaps to identify which of the statements reflect each of these feelings and behaviour states.

Activity sheet - Personal Conflict - your own story

This activity requires students to 'tell their own story' and to reflect upon a conflict that they have recently encountered with another pupil, adult or member of their family. They are asked in Part A of the sheet to describe this conflict. In Part B of the sheet they are asked to describe how they acted and to articulate what they said and did and Part C requires them to identify how the other person acted and what they said and did. Part D asks the question, 'What happened next?' Students are then asked to stop, think and reflect and to consider what they could have done or said differently in order to solve this conflict and what the other person involved could have done or said differently in order to solve the conflict and achieve a better outcome.

The emphasis is on being solution focused and identifying a way forward even when things seem quite difficult. Knowing how to behave, how to contain feelings, suspend anger and utilise the right words can reduce the level of conflict and ensure that it does not escalate further. It is helpful for this to be reinforced by the facilitator at the end of this activity when students can, if appropriate, feedback their responses. This will allow the facilitator to highlight any similarities or differences in the students' responses and to emphasise those that achieved or could have achieved better outcomes for the students involved.

Activity sheet - Conflict: The Results

This sheet is in fact an information sheet that provides students with information as to the three possible results of a conflict. These are as follows:

1) The problem is solved without violence:

- ▸ Both people co-operate and negotiate.
- ▸ Nobody is hurt.
- ▸ A compromise is reached.
- ▸ Both people can respect themselves and each other.

2) The problem is not solved because one person becomes aggressive and the other gives in:

- ▸ One person will get hurt.
- ▸ one person will get his or her own way.
- ▸ both people end up not respecting each other or themselves.

3) The problem is not solved because both people are aggressive:

- ▸ Both people get physically or emotionally hurt.
- ▸ Things end up worse than they were at the start.
- ▸ Both people end up not respecting each other or themselves.
- ▸ Nobody is a winner!

Students can discuss these three scenarios with the facilitator, and focus on why achieving a win/win situation (Number 1) is preferable to achieving a win/lose (Number 2) or lose/lose (Number 3) situation. The notions of co-operation and negotiation are central and these should be reinforced with students who should be clear about what each of these concepts means and involves. Understanding what a compromise is and how this can ensure respect is maintained is central to this activity.

To complete the information sheet, students can illustrate each of the possible outcomes.

Activity sheet - Top Tips for problem-solving

This final activity reinforces with students that if they wish to have a win/win solution to a conflict they need to make use of some of the following strategies:

- Walk away from the scene if it gets too hot.
- Make sure you take turns.
- Use 'I' messages.
- Go and get help when you think you need it.
- Compromise if necessary.
- Listen to the other person and let them have their say.
- Wait before opening your mouth or acting.
- Say how you feel and show you are sorry.
- Use problem-solving strategies.

Students are asked to highlight the strategies that they:

(a) make use of now

(b) don't make use of now and

(c) think that they might make use of in the future.

They can complete this on an individual basis and then feedback to the facilitator. You can highlight the strategies that most students seem to feel work best for them. It is helpful to ensure that students understand this notion of 'I' messages by providing some illustrated examples or role-play as appropriate, alongside reinforcing that more problem solving strategies will be introduced and consolidated in the subsequent session.

Plenary

The facilitator can utilise the whiteboard to scribe students' responses and feedback regarding the activities undertaken in this session. It is helpful to reinforce the win/win, win/lose, lose/lose outcomes and to highlight key vocabulary that students have learned during the session as follows:

- best possible outcome
- compromise
- conflict
- intimidation
- problem-solving
- respect
- self reflection
- solution
- assertive, aggressive and passive responses.

Games Activity - Handcuffs

In this activity, students require adequate space, time and a pair of ropes. They are required to stand in pairs. Each student has a rope tied carefully around her wrists to act as 'handcuffs'. However, prior to tying the 'handcuffs', the ropes are made to intertwine.

Scavenger Hunt

Look, stop, search and find:

Something edible.

Something you can write with.

Something that could light a fire.

Something pink.

Something from a bird.

Something that grows into a plant.

Something elastic.

Something perfectly round.

An item of rubbish.

Something that can be tied in a knot.

You're against the clock and the first team to find all ten win. Good luck!

Session 14

Emotional Literacy - Part One

Aims of the session

The facilitator can record the aims of the session on the whiteboard or flip-chart to facilitate the initial discussion and exploration of the concepts to be introduced. The main aims of the session are as follows:

- for students to identify the range of feelings that they currently experience on a daily basis and to categorise these in terms of comfort factors

- to identify and articulate emotional responses to a range of situations and to consider the extent to which these responses may or may not be person specific

- to increase awareness of an emotional vocabulary and the importance of developing the ability to articulate feelings successfully and appropriately

- for students to further understand the link between emotions and behaviours

- to identify negative emotional and behavioural patterns and ways in which these might be reduced, altered or eradicated.

This initial session on Emotional Literacy aims to impress on students the importance of developing and utilising an emotional vocabulary. This reinforces problem solving skills covered earlier and the idea that reflection and thinking before we act and speak is often the best way of achieving a positive and helpful outcome. To be able to articulate problems and associated feelings and describe behaviour in this way, we all need to have a sufficient emotional and descriptive vocabulary and be able to reflect upon our feelings and the way in which they impact upon our behaviours.

Activity sheet - Feeling the Facts

This activity aims to prompt students into considering the range of feelings that they may experience on a daily basis. Ask them to brainstorm the question: "How many feelings do you have?" Record their responses on the worksheet. Students can work in pairs for this activity or individually and this is entirely at the discretion of the facilitator. They should add up how many feelings they have recorded on the sheet and then sort them into three groups as follows: red = uncomfortable feelings; orange = both comfortable and uncomfortable; green = comfortable feelings. This can be done by highlighting each of the feelings recorded with the appropriate colour or by formulating three lists on the reverse of the activity sheet. It is helpful for the facilitator to discuss the notion of comfortable and uncomfortable feelings with the students prior to them undertaking this part of the activity. Providing an example as a prompt can help to promote students' thinking, such as feeling angry is usually an uncomfortable feeling, while feeling excited can be both comfortable and uncomfortable. Riding on a big dipper or watching a scary movie can be both a frightening and thrilling experience and this can be simultaneously comfortable and uncomfortable in terms of how we feel. Feeling happy and contented will usually be described as a comfortable feeling. The facilitator can ask students for feedback on this activity to raise awareness of these distinctions and to also highlight that our feelings can be both generalised and person specific. For example, what excites one person may not excite another and what makes one person feel sad and depressed may have little impact on someone else. Some situations engender very similar feelings in most people for example, bereavement will generally lead people to feel sad, distressed and upset if they have had a good or close relationship with the deceased.

Activity sheet - How Do You Feel?

This activity presents students with 12 scenarios that they can read through and then assess how they would feel in each of these situations. The emphasis is upon developing empathy and a vocabulary for our emotions.

Students are asked to work with a partner and to brainstorm ideas together. They are also asked to identify whether or not they would feel the same way as their partner or whether they would feel differently in each of these situations.

Activity sheet - Emotional Literacy Exercise

This is a seven-step activity which students are asked to work through on an individual basis. Consequently, it is helpful for students who find recording their ideas difficult to have access to a supportive peer or the facilitator.

Step 1	requires students to draw and label the four main feelings that they are most likely to experience in any school day.
Step 2	asks them to identify how they would behave or act when experiencing each of these feelings.
Step 3	then asks them to think about any unhelpful or negative behaviours that result from these feelings. They are asked to describe what is happening and why they feel this is the case. This is quite a difficult part of the activity and some students may require additional prompting and support in order to articulate this. However, it is crucial that they should begin to be able to reflect in this way since identifying unhelpful and negative behaviours is the first step in the process to eliminating them.
Step 4	asks students to think how they would like things to be different from in the initial scenario
Step 5	asks them to identify what they personally can do in order to make this happen. This is another way of identifying personal targets and can be reinforced in subsequent tutorial sessions.
Step 6	asks them to also identify what other people can do in order to make this happen. It is important to know that this can include both peers and adults in the school or learning community.
Step 7	asks pupils to answer the following questions: 'How will you feel if this does happen?' 'What will be different for you?'

This is a solution focused way of visualising the best possible outcome by a step approach and reinforces the cyclical nature of many of these activities as described in the introduction. For example:

- Self-reflection.

- What are my key skills?

- What goes well and why?

- What doesn't go well and why?

- How can I change unhelpful patterns of behaviour?

- Visualising and choosing new responses.

Plenary

The facilitator can act as a scribe for students' feedback on the activities undertaken in this session. Ideas can be recorded on the flip-chart or whiteboard as appropriate or the facilitator can lead or facilitate a discussion in which the main points are summarised or reinforced. In this initial session on Emotional Literacy, this concept will have been introduced mainly as an awareness of feelings and the need to distinguish between feelings and thoughts and actions. Students will have considered the link between their emotions and behaviours and the ways in which how they feel impacts upon their behaviour and their responses to others. The key notion is that negative behaviour patterns and feelings can be reduced or altered by being systematically self reflective and analytical. You can reinforce the key vocabulary covered and ensure that students have grasped concepts as follows:

- self reflection

- comfortable and uncomfortable distinction

- empathy

- person specific

- visualisation

- articulate

- empathise.

Games Activity - Water Torture

In keeping with theme of ESCAPE and survival, students are asked to work together in groups in order to carry an awkward item across an agreed route. This is an outside activity. The main purpose is to build up a sense of peer support and team working alongside reinforcing co-operation and empathy. Students will need a large bowl or heavy container filled with water. Students can also have access to some planks of wood for carrying purposes but only two per group. The 'winners' will be the group who manage to carry the container across the agreed route with minimal spillage and in the shortest time!

It would be helpful to reinforce group rules and the fact that all of these game activities reinforce the kinds of social and emotional skills that they will need in order to function appropriately within the mainstream context.

Finally, once students have completed the activity they can reflect upon it via the usual Circle Time approach, focusing on the following questions:

- How did we feel about this activity initially?
- What kinds of problems did we think would occur?
- What problems actually materialised?
- How did we deal with these difficulties?
- Could we have dealt with them more effectively?
- How will we deal with them better next time?
- What do we think we learnt from this activity?

Feeling the Facts

How many feelings do you have? Stop and think and record these below.

_____

_____

_____

_____

_____

_____

_____

_____

_____

_____

_____

_____

_____

_____

_____

_____

How many do you have?

Look at your list and sort these feelings into three groups:

       Red   uncomfortable feelings

       Orange   both comfortable and uncomfortable

       Green   comfortable feelings.

How Do You Feel?

How would you feel in each of these situations?

Your mum won't speak to you because you were late home.	Your form tutor has asked to see your parents because you were rude to him.	Your friend got £500 for her birthday from her dad whilst your dad gave you £20.
Someone is following you home late at night.	You came bottom in a maths test.	Your best friend has just been diagnosed with cancer.
You can't go on the trip because you hit your friend.	You've just won the lottery.	Your nan died last week and you really loved her.
You've just been given the chance to return to mainstream school.	Three older kids are bullying you and waiting for you at the gate.	A terrorist attack has just taken place and you have to evacuate the school building ASAP.

Work with a partner and brainstorm your ideas. Do you feel the same way as your partner or would you feel differently?

Emotional Literacy Exercise

Step (1) Draw and label the four main feelings you are most likely to experience in a school day.

Step (2) How do you behave or act when you experience each of these feelings?

Feeling (1)_____

Feeling (2)_____

Feeling (3)_____

Feeling (4)_____

Step (3)

Think about any unhelpful or negative behaviours. What is happening and why? (This is quite difficult so take your time.)

Emotional Literacy Excercise (2)

Step (4) Now think about how you would like things to be different.

Step (5) What can you do to make this happen?

Step (6) What can other people do to make this happen?

Step (7) How will you feel if this does happen?
What will be different for you?

Try it out! Go for it!

Session 15

Emotional Literacy - Part Two

Aims of the session

These can be recorded on the whiteboard by the facilitator prior to the start of the session. This will enable students to clarify expectations of the session and articulate any questions or concerns that they may have at the outset. The aims of the session are as follows:

- for students to understand further the concept of Emotional Literacy and the key skills which make an emotionally literate person

- for students to analyse and reflect upon their own skills in the area of Emotional Literacy

- for students to understand and assess their own key skills and the importance of developing these further in order to specifically develop and maintain positive relationships alongside achieving further success in both the academic and social context

- for students to consider and summarise the key skills and concepts covered in the course as a whole alongside evaluating the course and its usefulness to them on an individual basis.

The central aim of this programme is to have developed students' Emotional Literacy and their ability to recognise, understand, handle and appropriately express their feelings. Students need to be able to understand that developing such skills is a key to success both academically and socially. Developing these skills provides them with the 'toolbox' necessary in order to escape and return to the mainstream context.

Activity sheet - More Emotional Literacy

This information sheet provides students with two definitions of Emotional Literacy as follows:

- 'Emotional Literacy is the ability to recognise, understand, handle and appropriately express feelings - both your own and those of other people.'

- 'People who are emotionally literate are able to get on with others, resolve conflicts, motivate themselves and achieve in life.'

The facilitator can read these out to students and encourage them to discuss each statement in turn. It can be pointed out that the whole purpose of this course has been to enable students to develop these specific skills and to also be able to transfer these into a range of other contexts.

The second part of the information sheet details key skills in Emotional Literacy as follows:

- awareness of feelings
- personal insight
- self-assurance
- self-regulation
- authenticity
- accountability
- flexibility
- self motivation.

These are the key skills that have been focused upon during the ESCAPE course and hopefully, students will have begun to develop their skills in each of the key areas. At this point students can either work in a pair or as a member of the whole group in order to formulate their own definitions for each of these key skills. Dictionaries and thesauruses should be made available in order to prompt students in this activity. Students can record their definitions on the Emotional Literacy sheet.

Activity sheet - Emotional Literacy Dictionary: our own definitions

This sheet provides a format in which students can record their definitions of each of the key skills. Students can work in a pair to ensure that those whose literacy skills are not highly developed are adequately supported. They can then relate their definitions to the course facilitator and compare these with other pairs in the group. The course facilitator can scribe ideas onto the whiteboard and attempt to help the students formulate definitions for each of the key skills that are owned by the whole group.

Activity sheet - How is your Emotional Literacy?

Students are then asked to complete their own personal assessment as to the current level of their Emotional Literacy skills. They are asked to rate themselves on each of the key skills identified in the initial activity on a scale of 0-5. (0 = never, 3 = average, 5 = always). The facilitator should assist students whose literacy skills are not deemed to be adequate. This activity is intended as one of personal reflection and it is not anticipated that students should be required to feedback on this to the group as a whole. The idea is to encourage students to self-reflect and to then identify areas in which they may like to further develop their skills in the future.

Activity sheet - Emotional Literacy Target Skills

Students are finally asked to rate themselves on each of the eight key areas of Emotional Literacy on a scale of 1-10. (1 = never, 5 = sometimes, 10 = always). Once this has been completed they are then asked to work out a personal target for each area in order to further improve their skills. This target sheet can then be taken to subsequent tutorial sessions and discussed and further analysed. This particular format may also be a useful tool for measuring progress at a later date, that is, students may wish to review their personal Emotional Literacy targets after two weeks, one month or two months. This can be done either in the current context or in the mainstream context, allowing for an assessment as to how well skills have been transferred and further developed.

Plenary

The facilitator can act as a scribe here in terms of reviewing not only the content of this session but also the content of the course as a whole and what skills and strategies students feel that they have been able to learn and absorb during the time allocated. The main concepts covered can be recorded, for example, Emotional Literacy including awareness of feelings, personal insight, self-assurance, self-regulation, authenticity, accountability, flexibility, self motivation, locus of control, anger management, assertiveness, stress management, self-esteem, survival techniques, empathy and problem-solving skills.

Students may wish to focus on key vocabulary alongside key skills learnt and covered prior to finally completing the evaluation of the ESCAPE course. It is important for students to realise the depth and importance of the work that they have undertaken and the need to ensure that they are able to confidently incorporate these skills and strategies into their daily lives. Finally, it is vital that they provide an honest evaluation for the course facilitator to ensure the usefulness and appropriateness of the course materials and contents for future sessions and courses. The evaluation worksheet asks students to rate themselves on a scale of 1-10 for how they feel about specific areas (1 = not good or useful, 5 = okay or quite useful, 10 = excellent or extremely useful).

Finally, students are asked to answer the following questions:

▸ If you were running this course or participating in it again, what changes would you make?

▸ Would you change the delivery, the structure or content of the sessions?

Games Activity - Walk the Plank

In this activity, students require adequate space, time and a large plank per group. They are required to stand on the plank or piece of paper and to then respond to the directions given by the course facilitator. The directions will all involve sorting ideas such as sort into alphabetical order, height order or age order. This activity may need to take place outside of the classroom context depending on the size of the group. This activity aims to promote and reinforce student's ability to co-operate effectively. It is also intended to generate a sense of personal space and improve students' ability to negotiate and relax within this space.

Finally, once students have completed the activity they can reflect upon it via the usual Circle Time approach, focusing on the following questions:

▸ How did we feel about this activity initially?

▸ What kinds of problems did we think would occur?

▸ What problems actually materialised?

▸ How did we deal with these difficulties?

▸ Could we have dealt with them more effectively?

▸ How will we deal with them better next time?

▸ What do we think we learnt from this activity?

▸ It might be useful to ask the students not to use any verbal communication.

Emotional Literacy Exercise

'Emotional Literacy is the ability to recognise, understand, handle and appropriately express feelings-both your own and those of other people.'

'People who are emotionally literate are able to get on with others, resolve conflicts, motivate themselves and achieve in life.'

Key skills in Emotional Literacy:

▶ Awareness of feelings.

▶ Personal insight.

▶ Self-assurance.

▶ Self-regulation.

▶ Authenticity.

▶ Accountability.

▶ Flexibility.

▶ Self-motivation.

Work with a partner to try and formulate your own definition for each key skill listed above. Use a dictionary and thesaurus to help. Record your definitions on the Emotional Literacy Dictionary sheet.

Emotional Literacy Dictionary

(Our own definitions)

Accountability	Personal insight
Authenticity	Self-assurance
Awareness of feelings	Self-motivation
Flexibility	Self-regulation

How is your Emotional Literacy?

How do you rate? Read each statements and tick against each scale from:

1 = never   3 = average   5 = always

Key skill 1 - Awareness of your own feelings

You know what you are feeling.

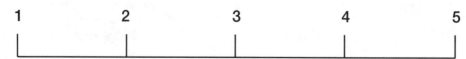

You can label your feelings.

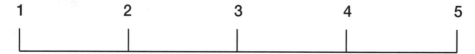

You know when your feelings affect your work.

You know when your feelings affect your relationships.

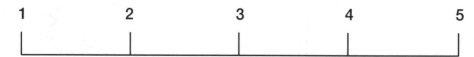

Key skill 2 - Personal Insight

You know your strengths.

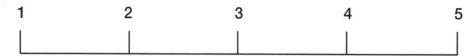

You know your weaknesses.

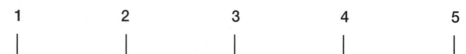

You can take constructive criticism and feedback form others.

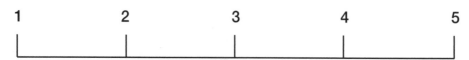

You don't take yourself too seriously.

```
1          2          3          4          5
|_____|_____|_____|_____|
```

You know when you've done something well and can feel good about yourself.

```
1          2          3          4          5
|_____|_____|_____|_____|
```

Key skill 3 - Self-assurance

You act confidently in most situations.

```
1          2          3          4          5
|_____|_____|_____|_____|
```

You stick up for things you think are right.

```
1          2          3          4          5
|_____|_____|_____|_____|
```

Other people think you are confident.

```
1          2          3          4          5
|_____|_____|_____|_____|
```

Key skill 4 - Self-regulation and control

You can stop yourself when you know you've behaving in a way that will cause problems (for you and others).

```
1          2          3          4          5
|_____|_____|_____|_____|
```

You can keep calm under pressure.

```
1          2          3          4          5
|_____|_____|_____|_____|
```

You can handle uncomfortable feelings and use strategies to reduce stress and anxiety.

```
1          2          3          4          5
|_____|_____|_____|_____|
```

Key skill 5 - Authenticity

When you say you'll do something, you'll do it.

1	2	3	4	5

You don't say or act one thing and then do another.

1	2	3	4	5

You can admit your mistakes.

1	2	3	4	5

You can stand up for what you think even if you are in the minority.

1	2	3	4	5

Key skill 6 - Accountability

You can take responsibility for your behaviour and actions.

1	2	3	4	5

You keep your promises.

1	2	3	4	5

You admit it when you have made a mistake.

1	2	3	4	5

Key skill 7 - Flexibility

You can cope with changes to your day.

1	2	3	4	5

You don't get stressed by change and can go with the flow.

1   2   3   4   5

You like to be creative and think of new ways of doing things.

1   2   3   4   5

Key skill 8 - Self-motivation

You like to achieve your best.

1   2   3   4   5

You like to get things done.

1   2   3   4   5

You are committed to your relationships.

1   2   3   4   5

You'll keep going even if things get tough.

1   2   3   4   5

You are optimistic and look for opportunities before you look for a problem.

1   2   3   4   5

You can handle uncomfortable feelings and use strategies to reduce stress and anxiety.

1   2   3   4   5

Stop and think!

Where are your highest scores? Where are your lowest scores?

Which is your best key skill and which is your weakest?

Emotional Literacy Target Skills

Rate yourself overall for each key skill (on a scale of 1-10

    1 = never   5 = sometimes   10 = always).

Then try to work out a personal target for each area in order to further improve your skills.

Key skills	Rating	Personal Target
Awareness of feelings		
Personal insight		
Self-assurance		
Self-regulation		
Authenticity		
Accountability		
Flexibility		
Self-motivation		

Evaluation of ESCAPE Course

Please help us to help you!

Overall, rate yourself on a scale of 1-10, for how you feel about the following areas:

1 = not good/useful   5 = OK/quite useful   10 = excellent/extremely useful

☐	Escape group sessions.
☐	Games activities.
☐	Tutorial sessions.
☐	The topics covered.
☐	Effect on self-esteem.
☐	Effect on my confidence.
☐	Effect on my ability to manage angry feelings.
☐	Effect on my ability to manage my behaviour.
☐	Effect on my ability to empathise with others.
☐	The level of my emotional literacy overall.
☐	The materials presented in the programme.
☐	The discussion element of each session.
☐	The way in which sessions were presented by the course facilitator.
☐	The way in which the course facilitator interacted with me and supported me during the course.
☐	How the course made me feel about my future and myself.

If you were running this course or participating in it again, what changes would you make? Would you change the delivery, the structure or content of the session? Record you ideas and thoughts below.

Don't forget to visit our website for all our latest publications, news and reviews.

www.luckyduck.co.uk

New publications every year on our specialist topics:

- **Emotional Literacy**
- **Self-esteem**
- **Bullying**
- **Positive Behaviour Management**
- **Circle Time**
- **Anger Management**
- **Asperger's Syndrome**
- **Eating Disorders**

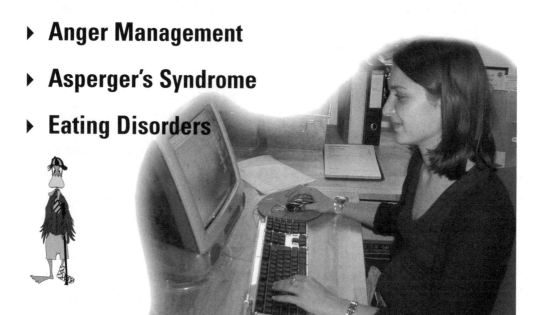